NYC DECK
Daniel Newman

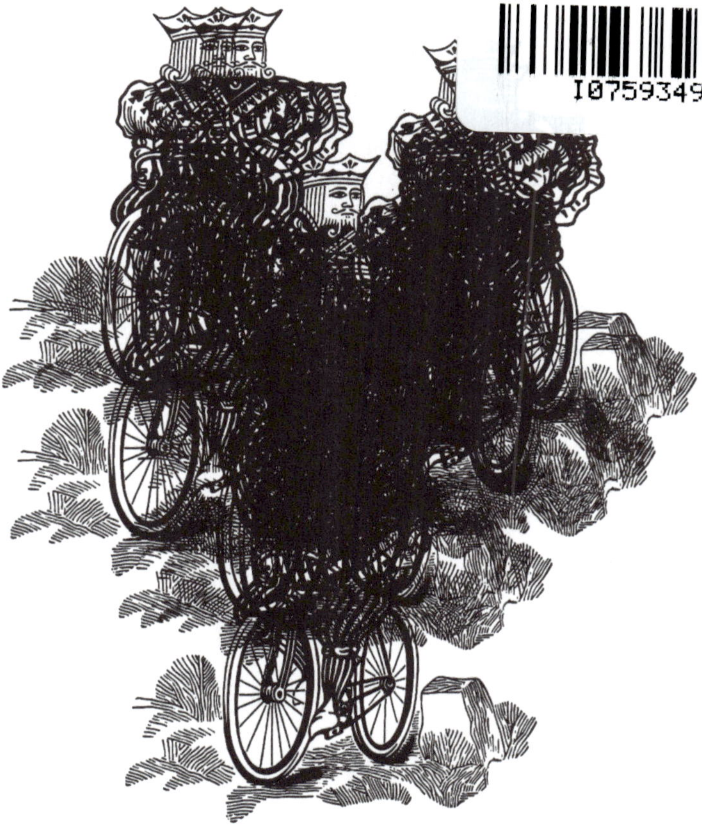

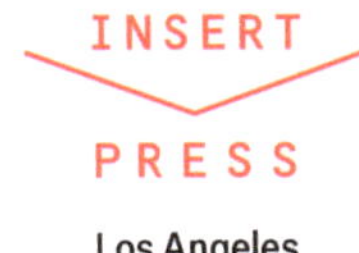

INSERT
PRESS

Los Angeles

Insert Press

ISBN: 978-1-947322-03-5
Library of Congress Control Number: 2022944688

Design and Layout by Mathew Timmons.
Inside front cover design by Matt Normand.

NYC Deck documents a multi-year project in which the artist Daniel Newman collected an entire deck of playing cards one-by-one over an extended period of time, on the streets and in the gutters of New York City.

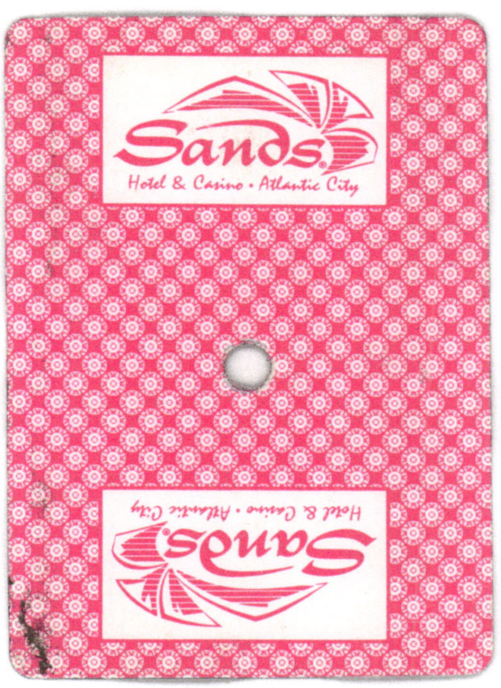
Sands
Hotel & Casino · Atlantic City
Sands
Hotel & Casino · Atlantic City

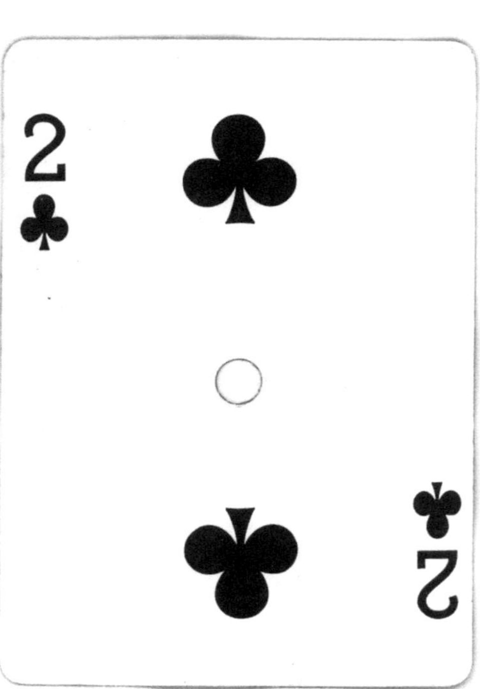

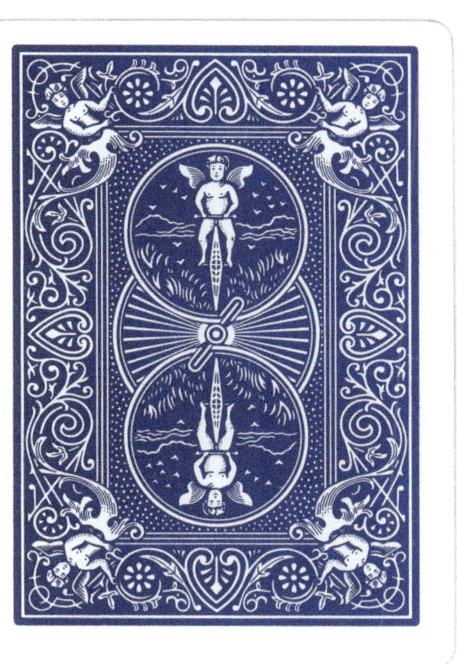

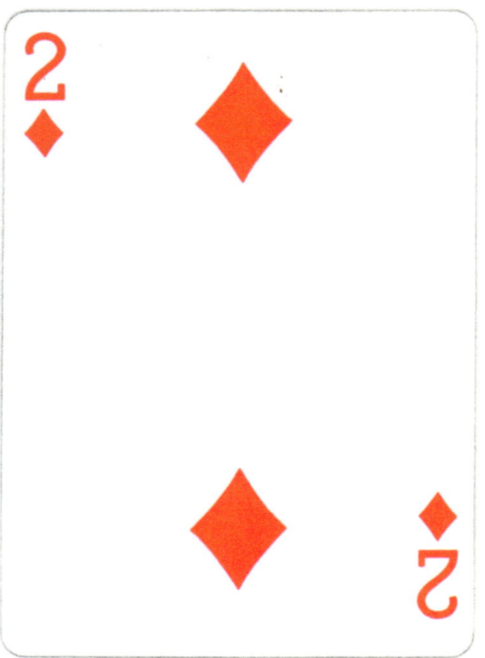

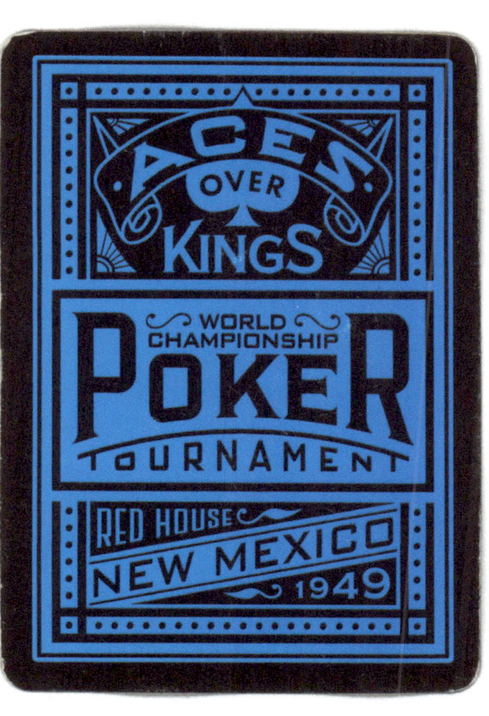

ACES
OVER
KINGS
WORLD
CHAMPIONSHIP
POKER
TOURNAMENT
RED HOUSE
NEW MEXICO
1949

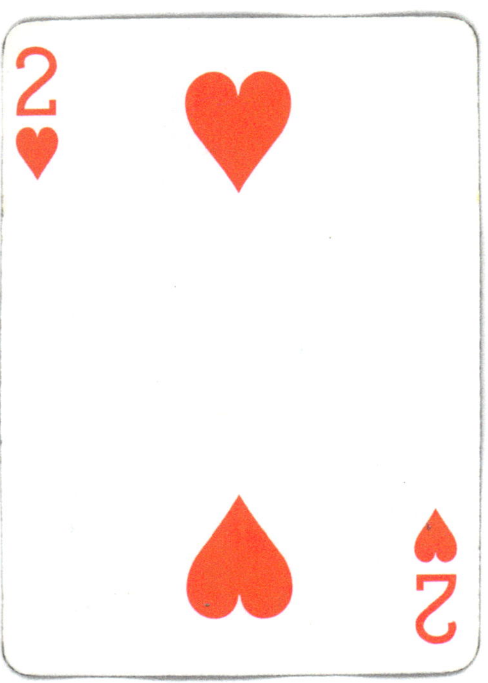

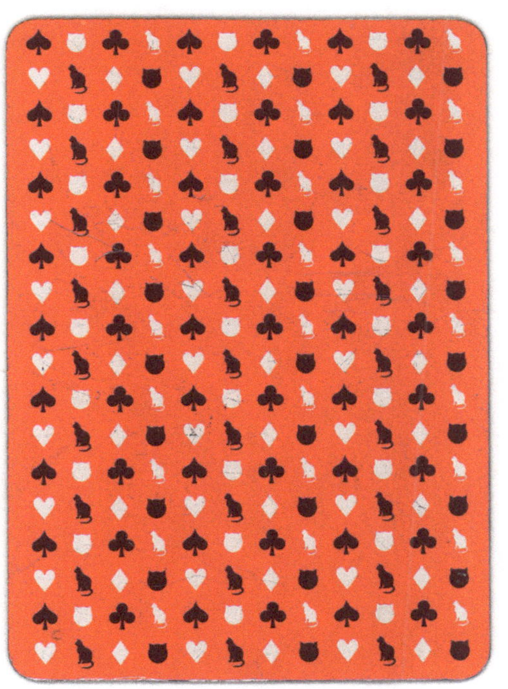

2 ♠

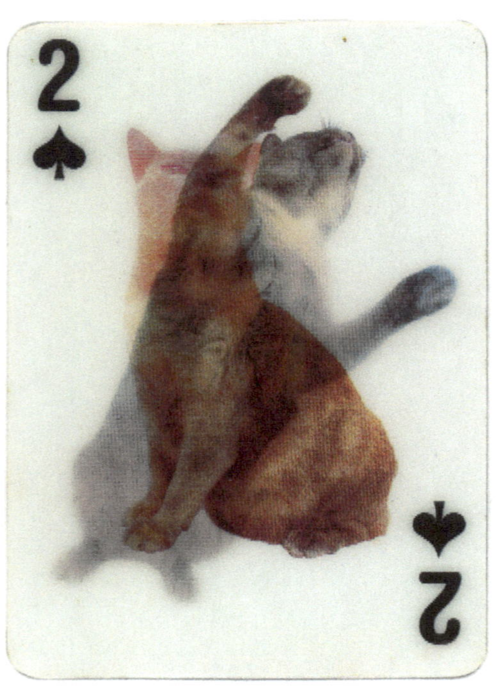

2 ♠

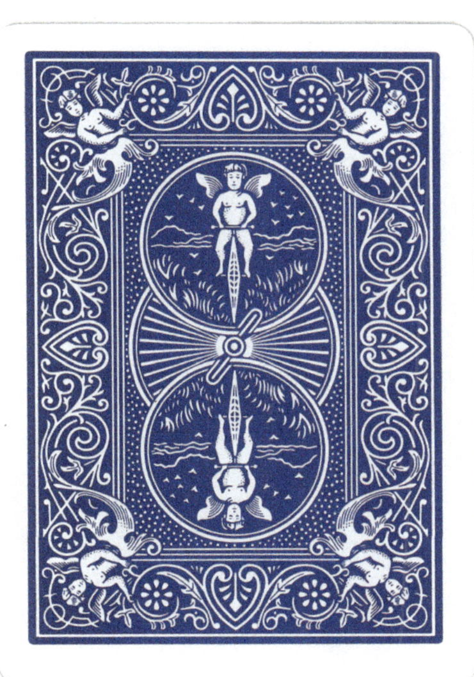

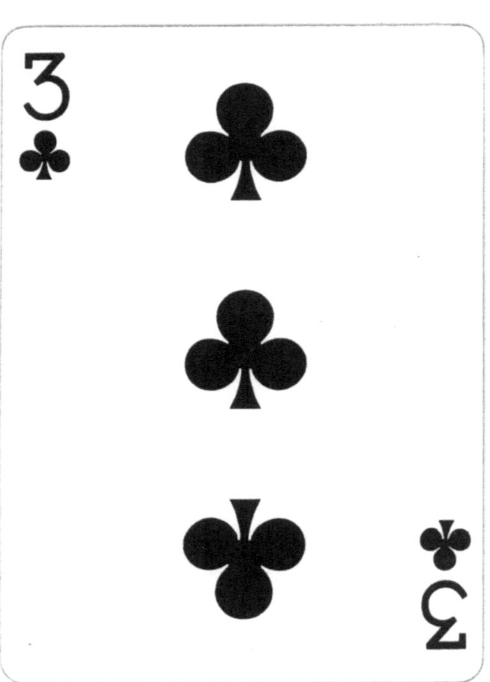

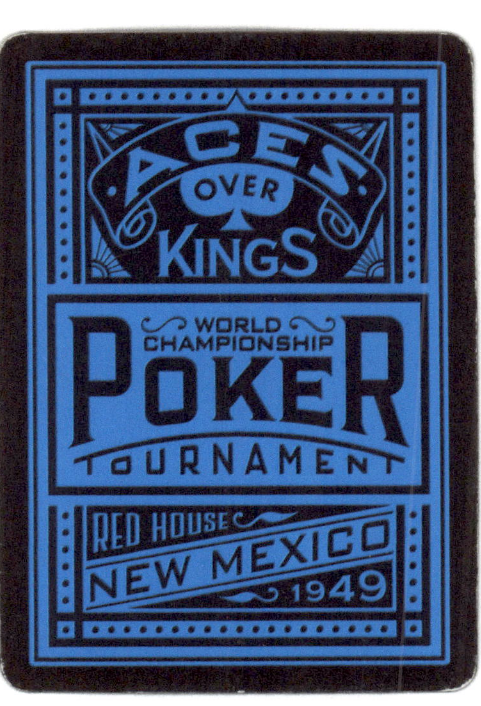

ACES
OVER
KINGS
WORLD
CHAMPIONSHIP
POKER
TOURNAMENT
RED HOUSE
NEW MEXICO
1949

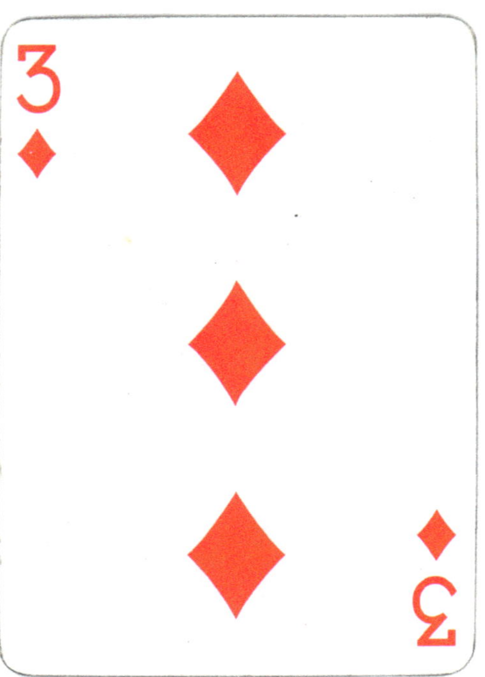

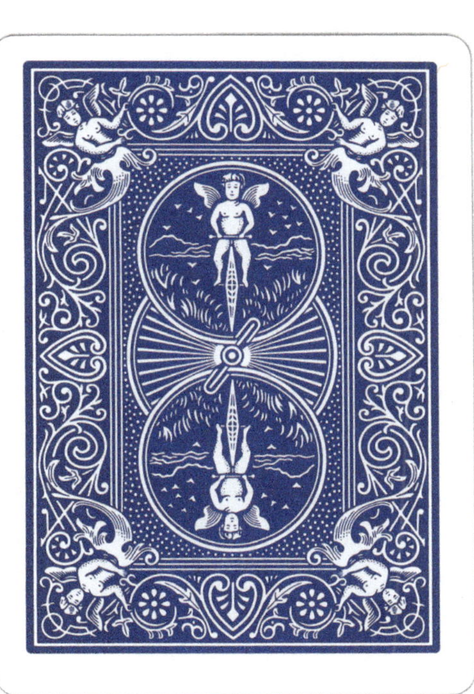

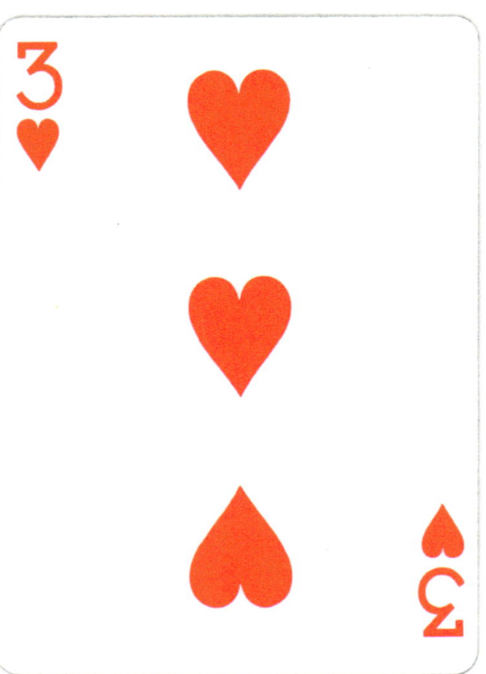

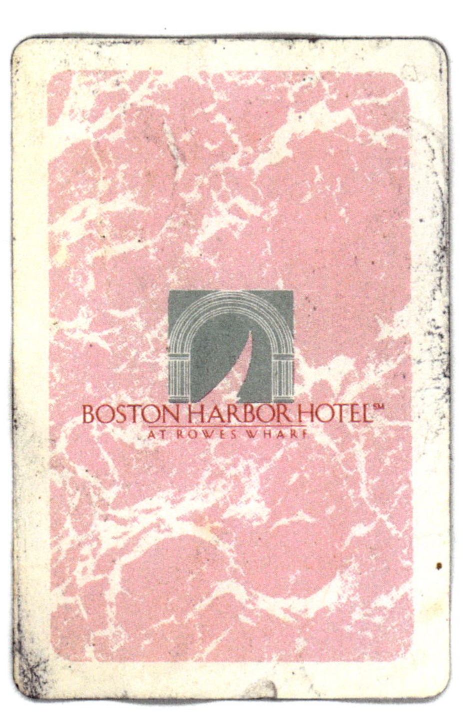

BOSTON HARBOR HOTEL℠
AT ROWES WHARF

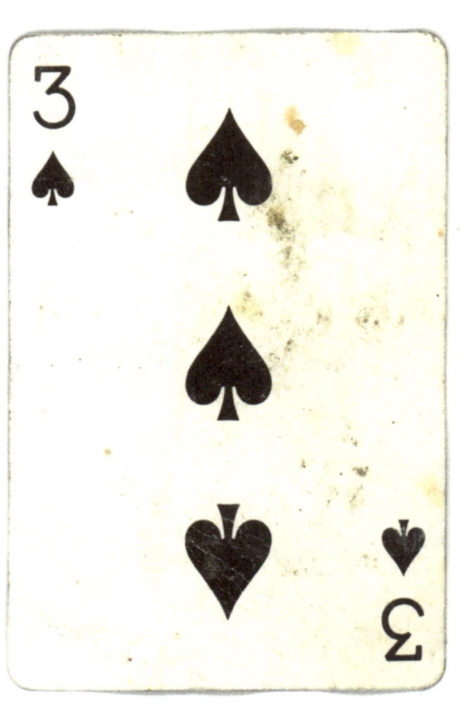

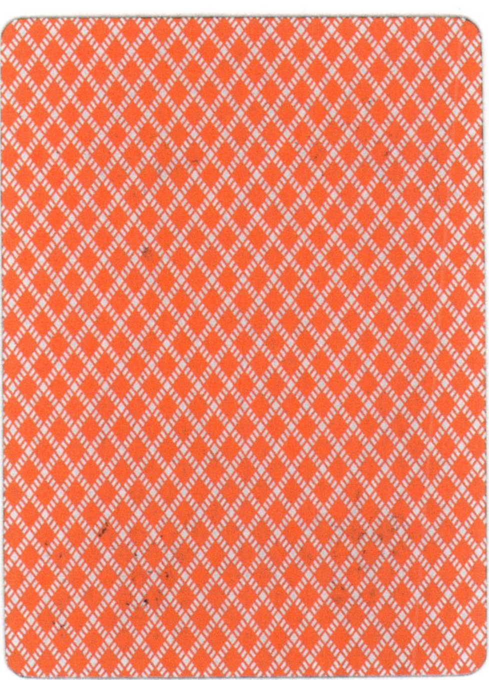

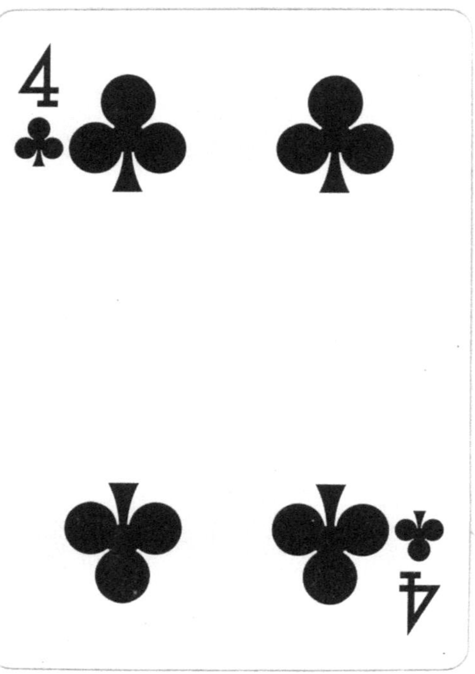

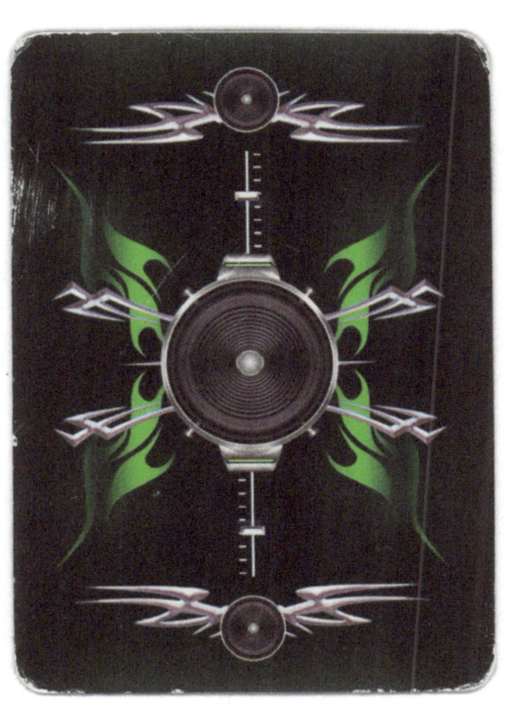

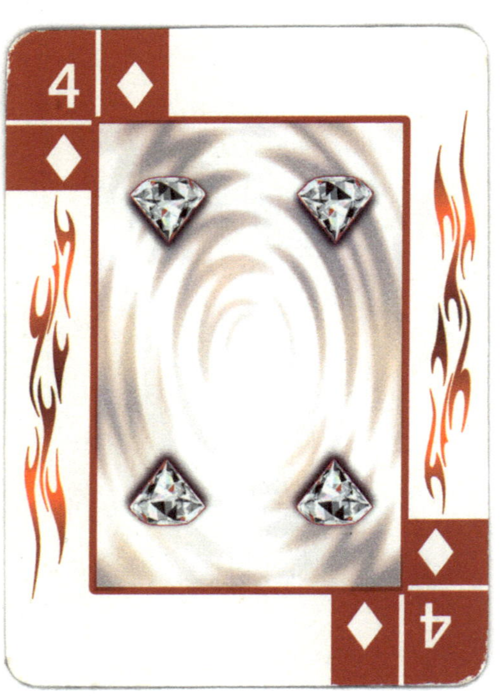

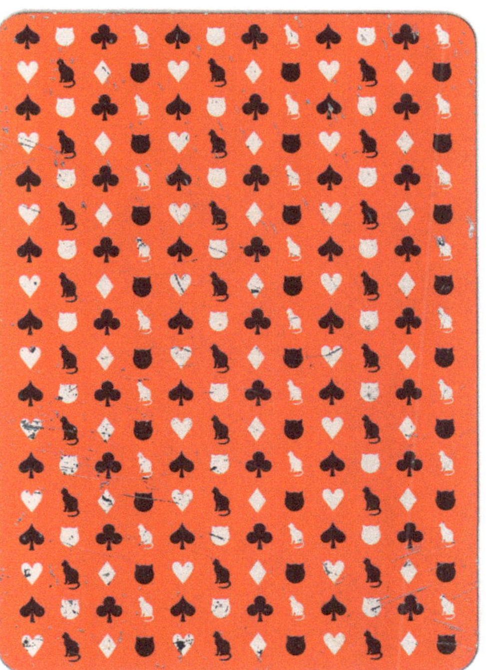

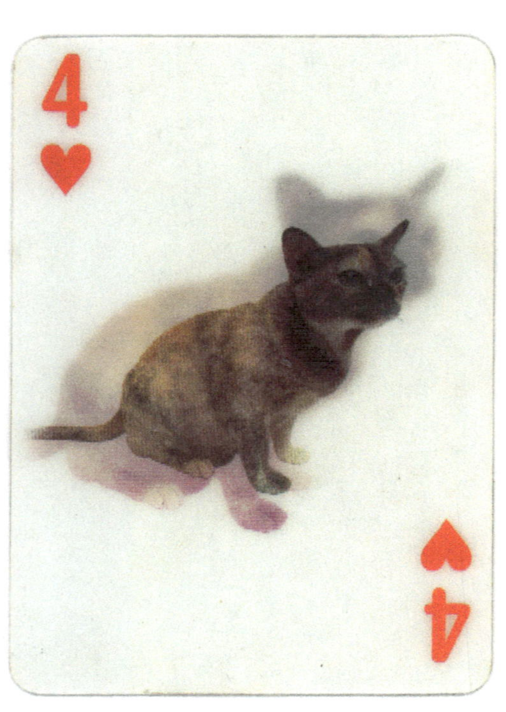

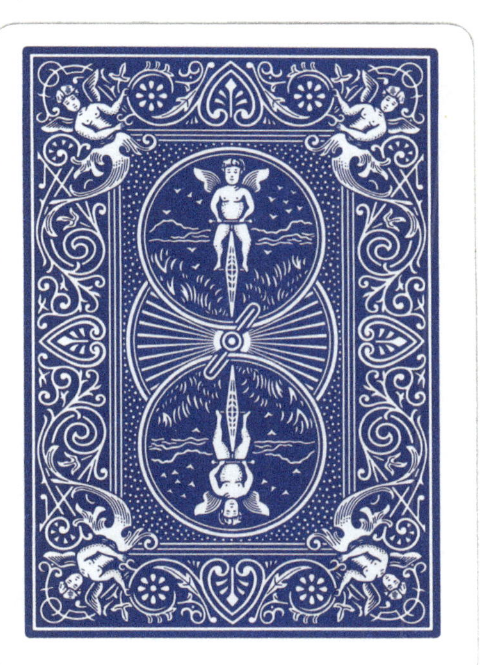

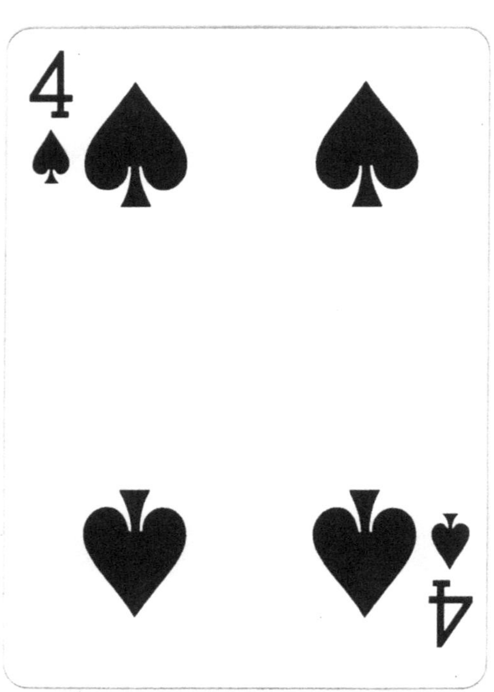

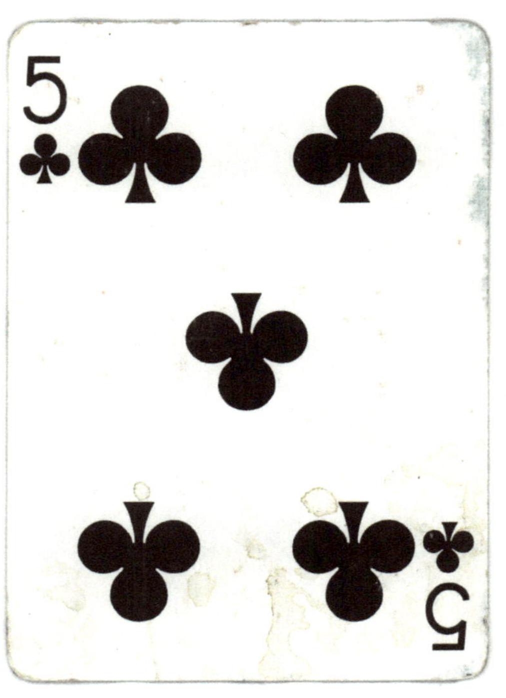

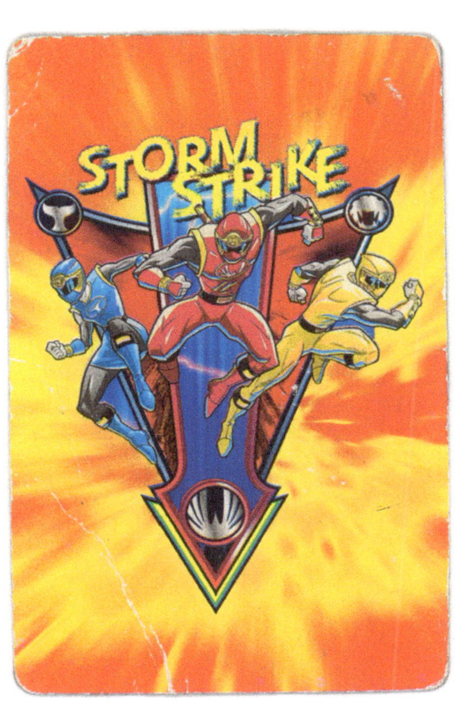

STORM
STRIKE

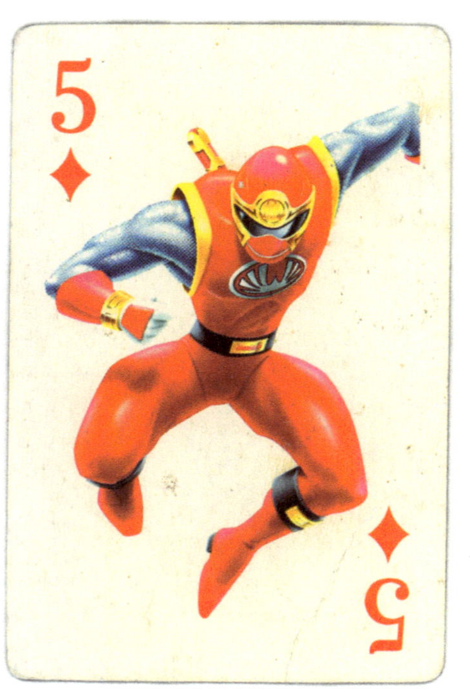

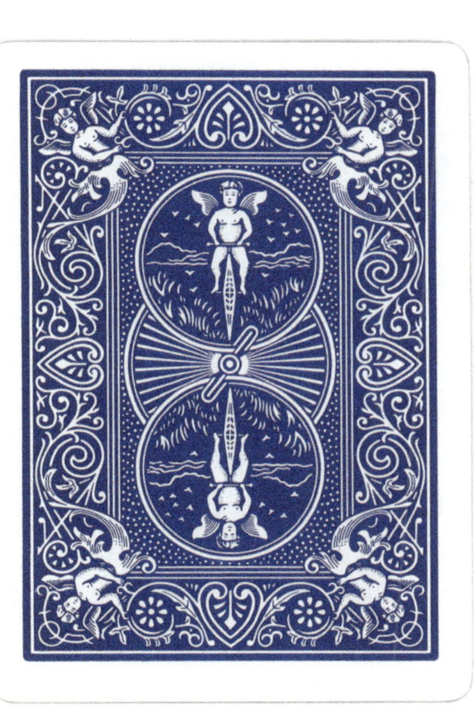

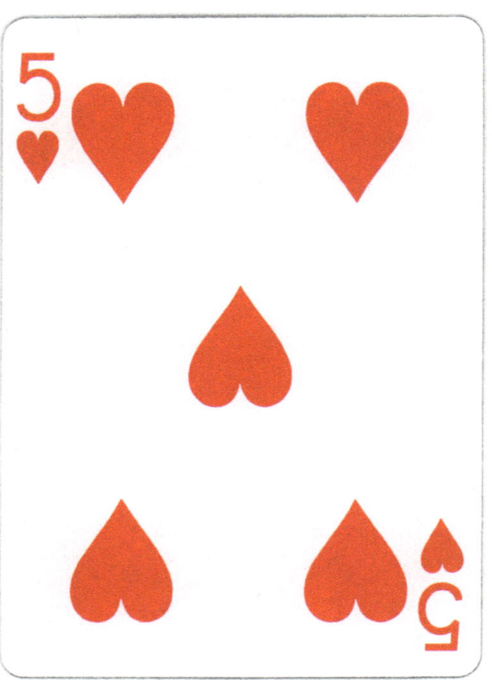

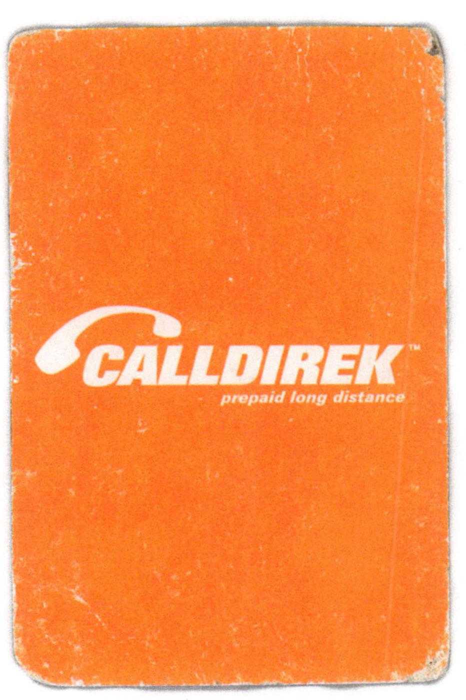
CALLDIREK
prepaid long distance

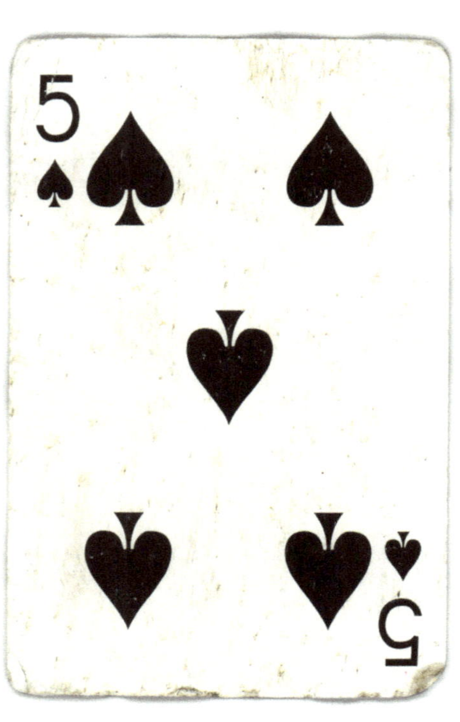

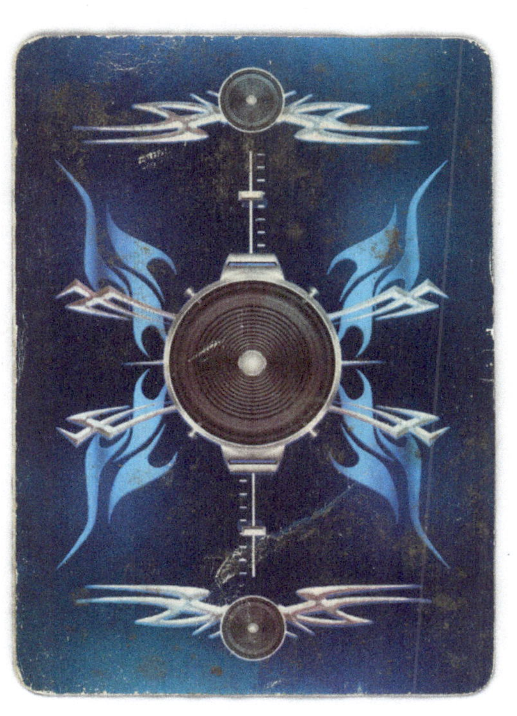

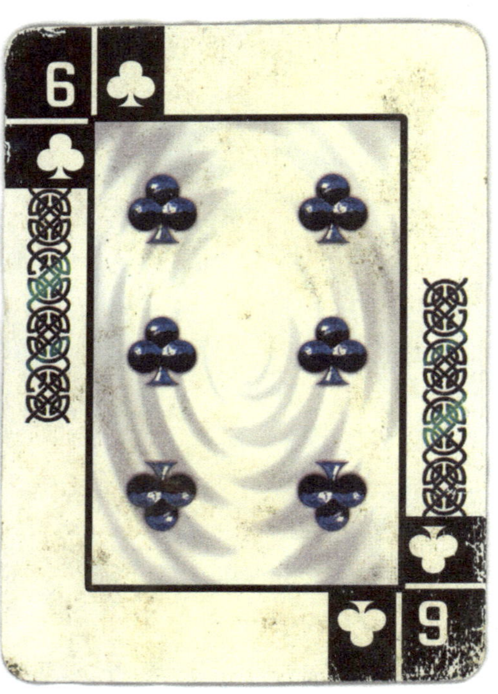

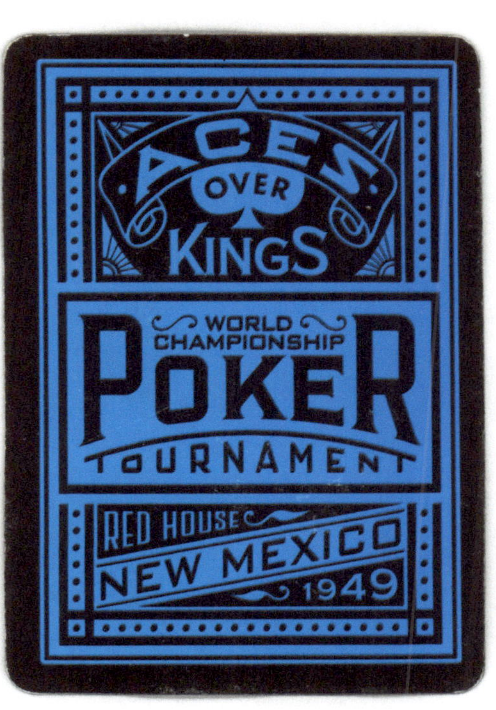

ACES
OVER
KINGS
WORLD CHAMPIONSHIP
POKER
TOURNAMENT
RED HOUSE
NEW MEXICO
1949

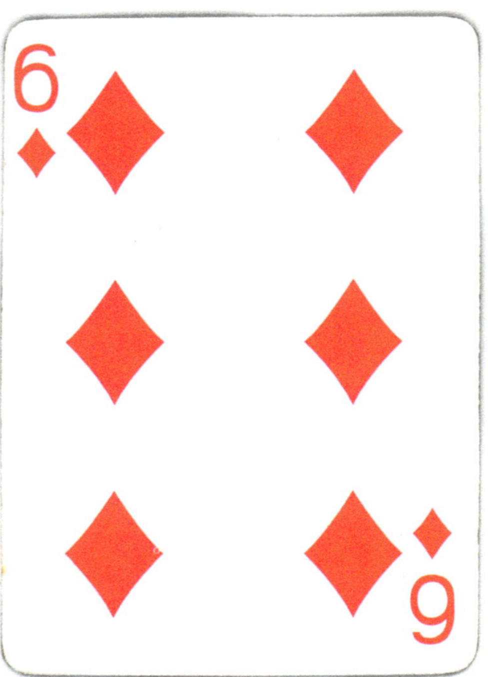

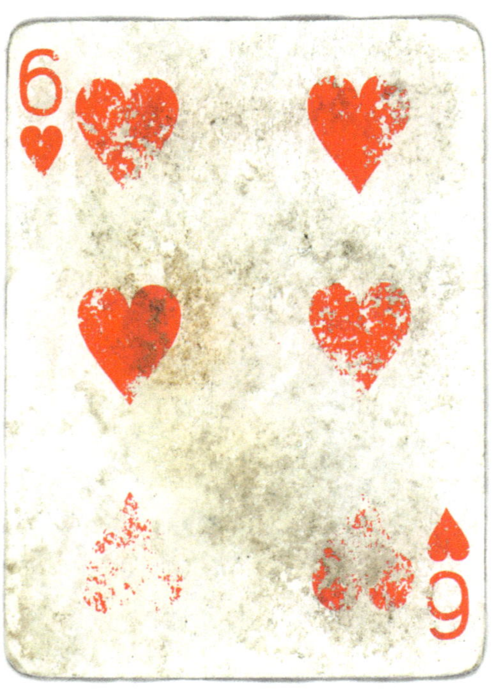

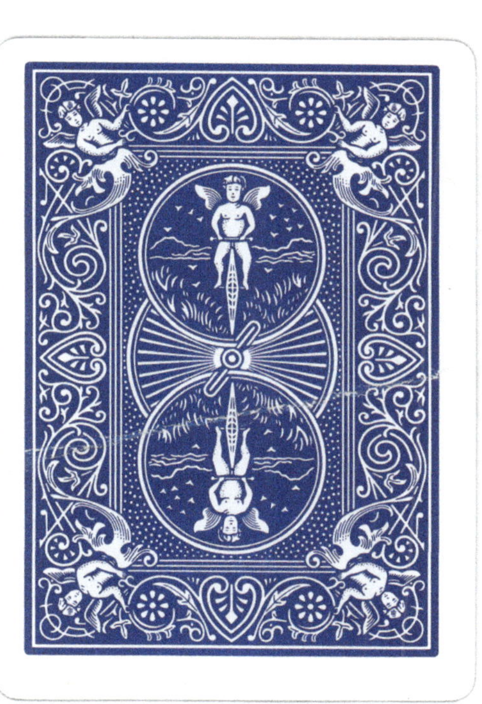

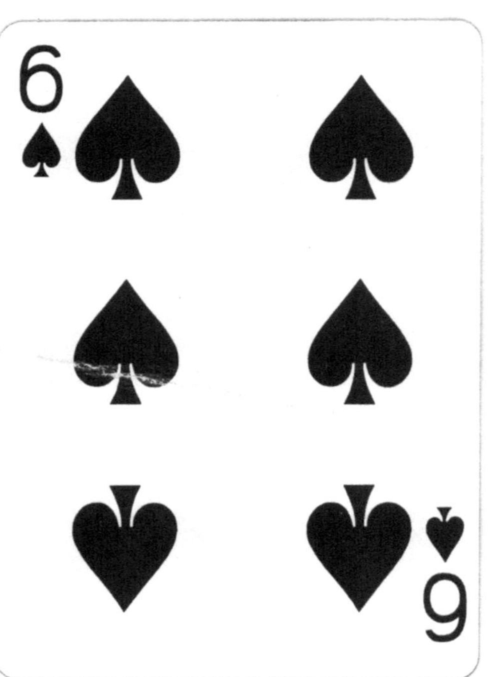

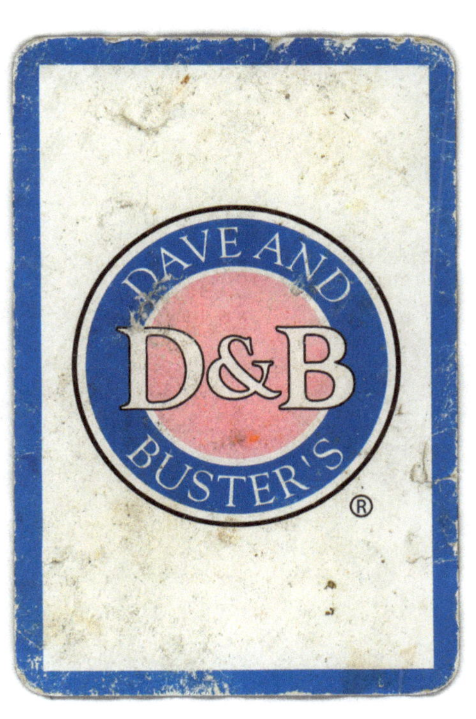
DAVE AND
BUSTER'S
D&B
®

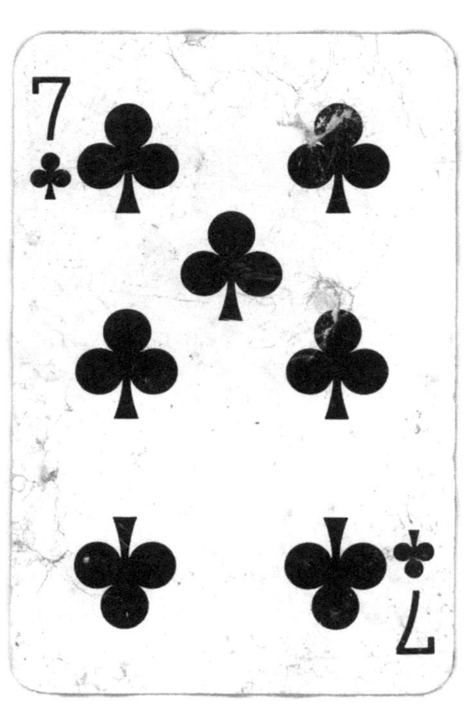

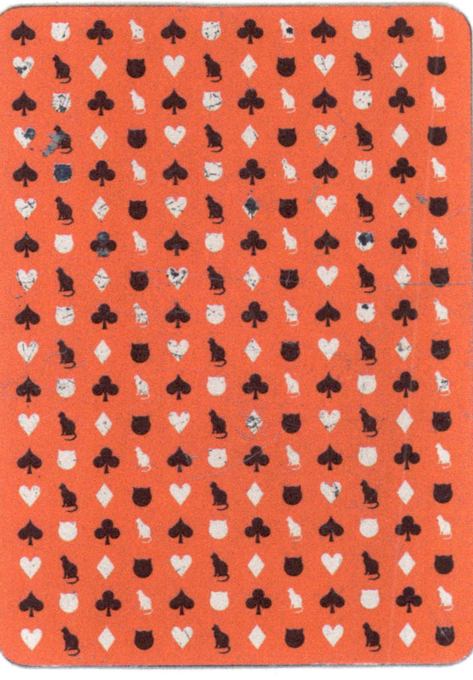

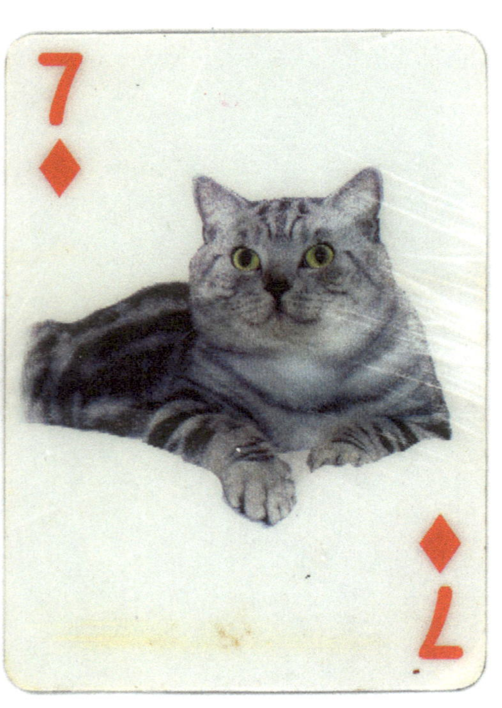

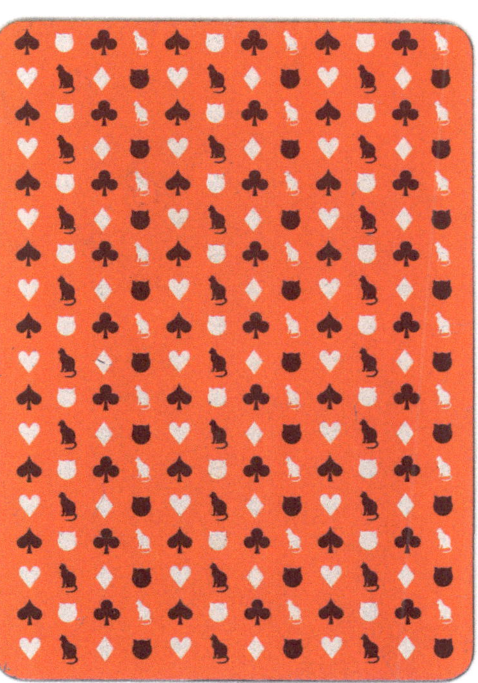

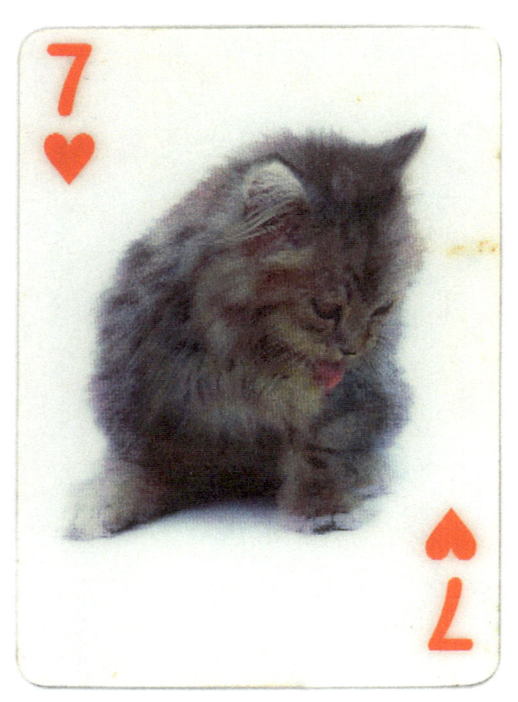

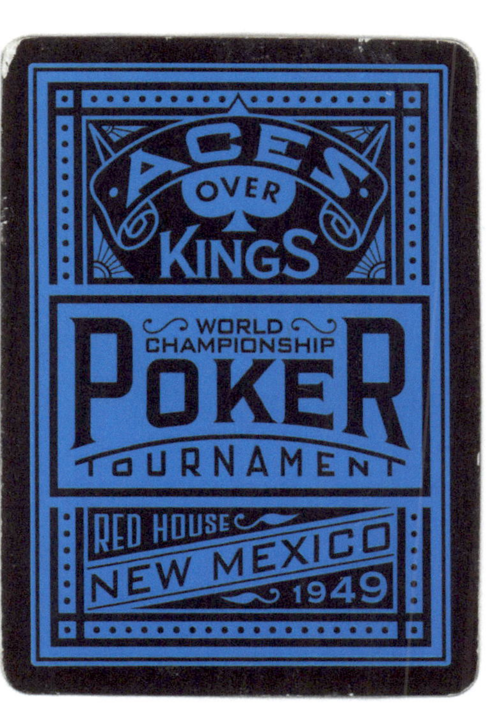

ACES
OVER
KINGS
WORLD
CHAMPIONSHIP
POKER
TOURNAMENT
RED HOUSE
NEW MEXICO
1949

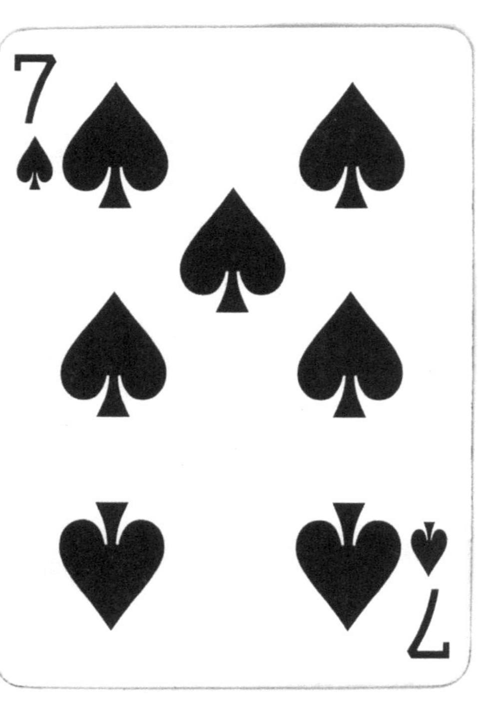

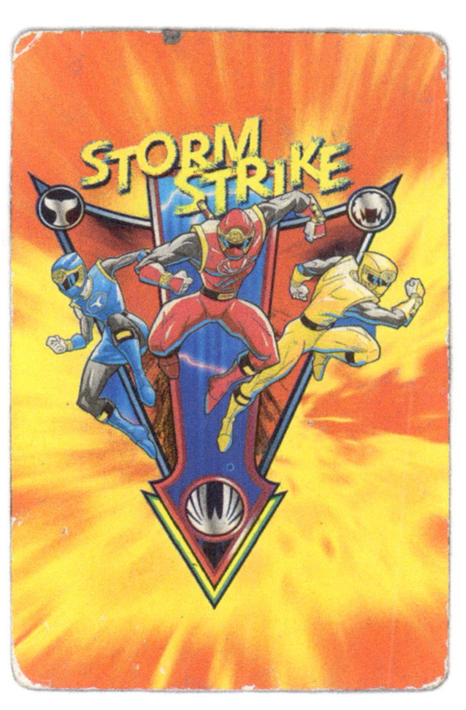

STORM
STRIKE

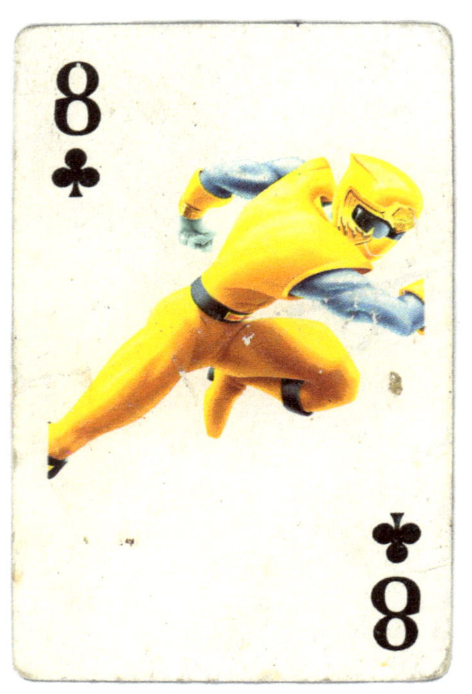

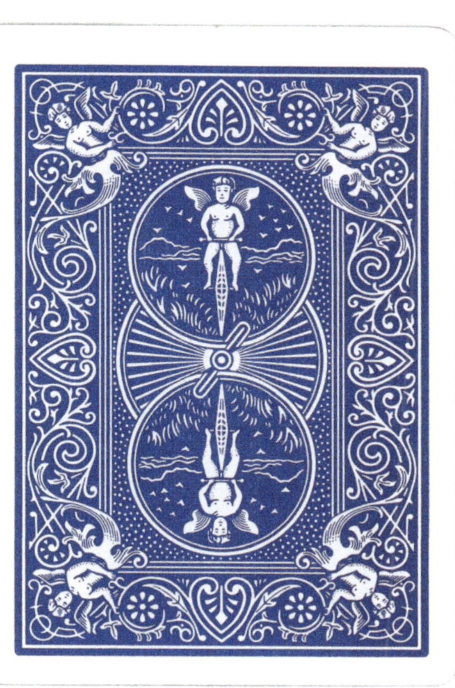

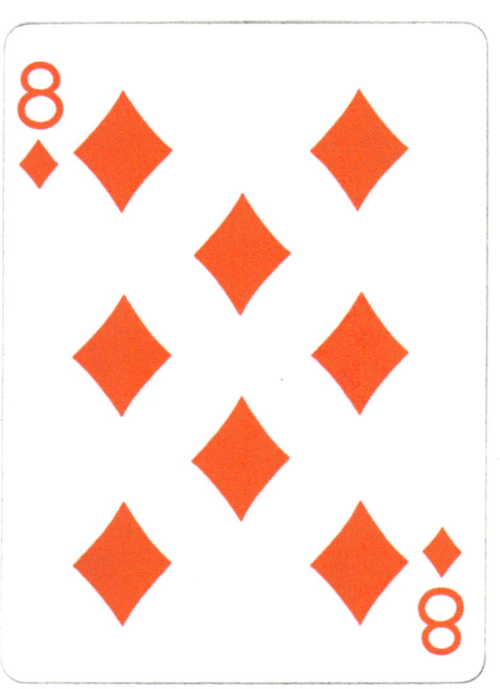

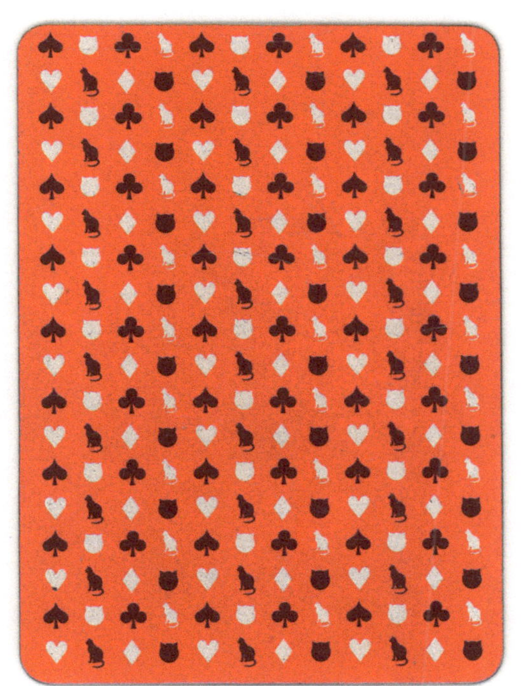

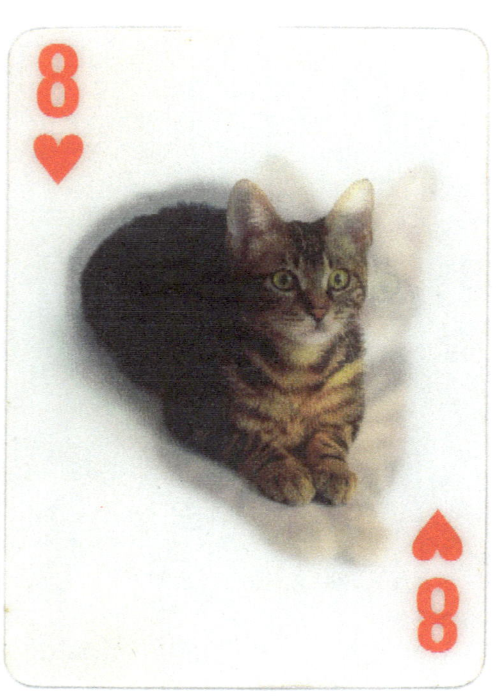
8
8

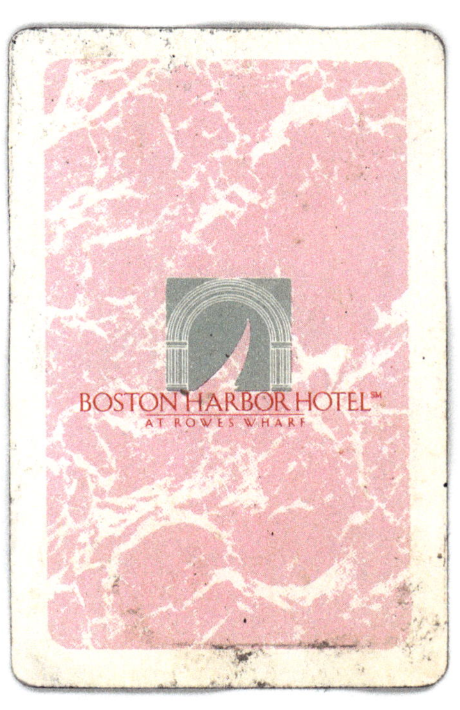
BOSTON HARBOR HOTEL℠
AT ROWES WHARF

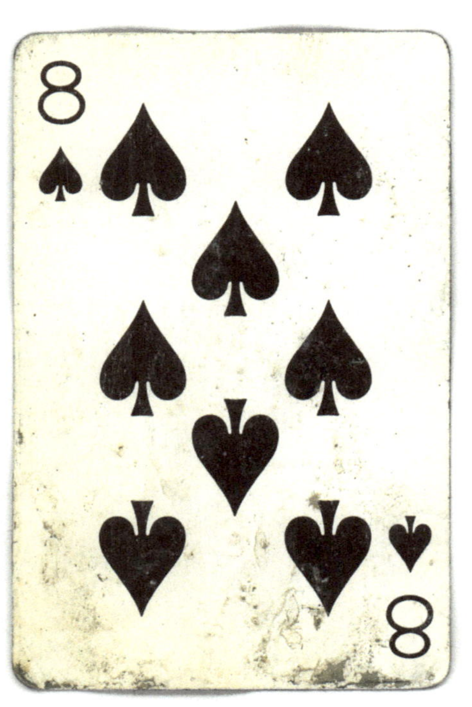

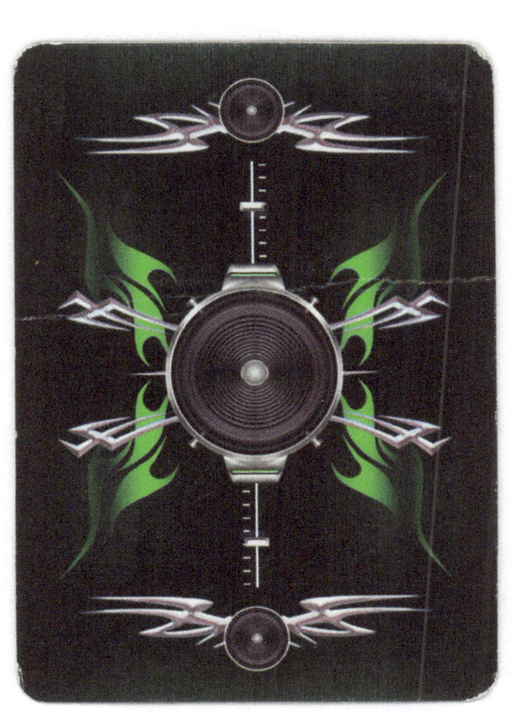

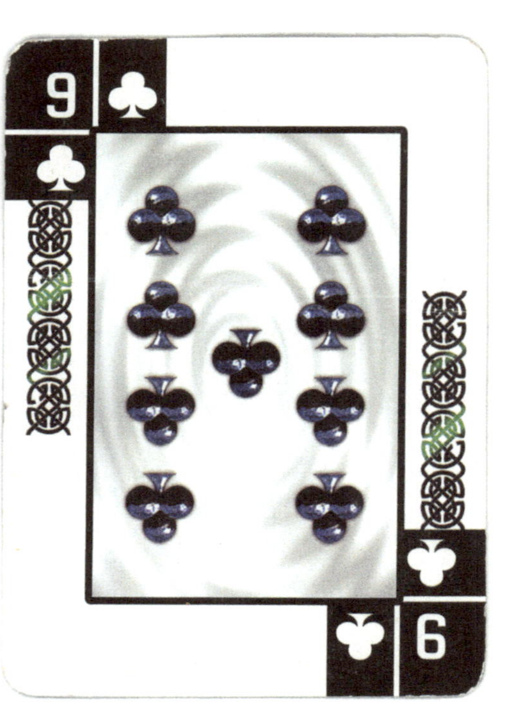

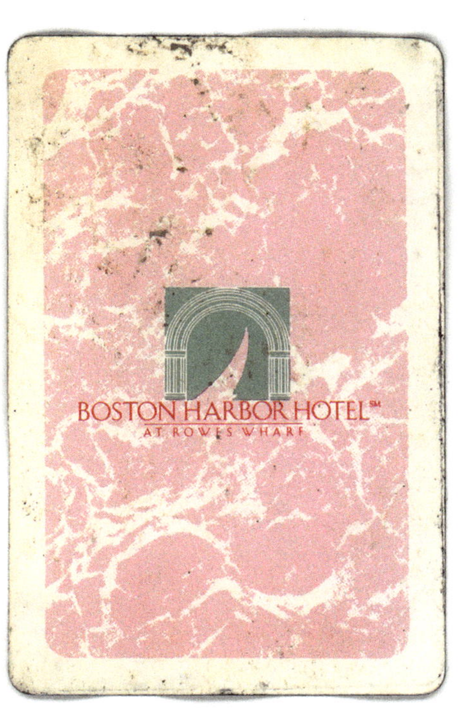

BOSTON HARBOR HOTEL℠
AT ROWES WHARF

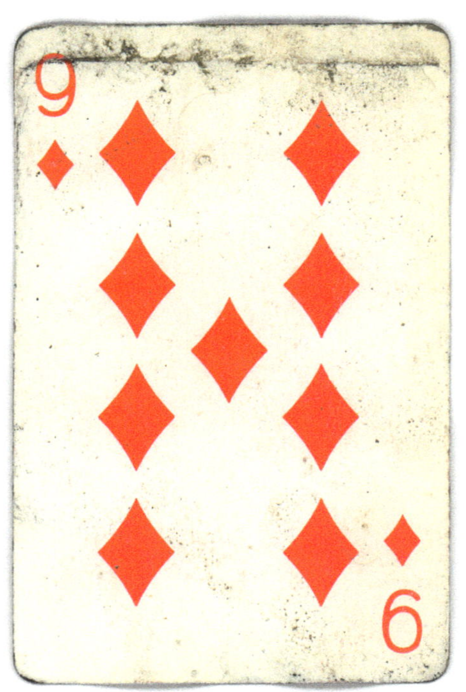

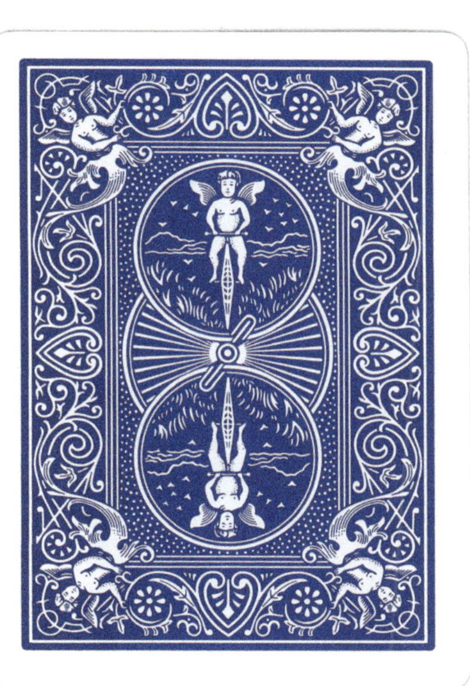

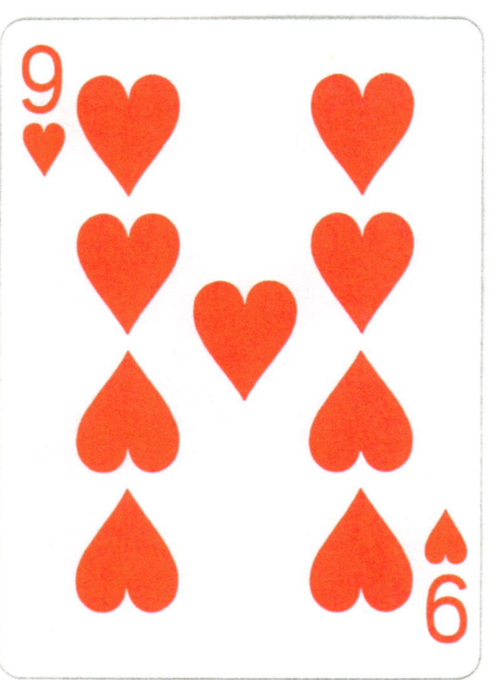

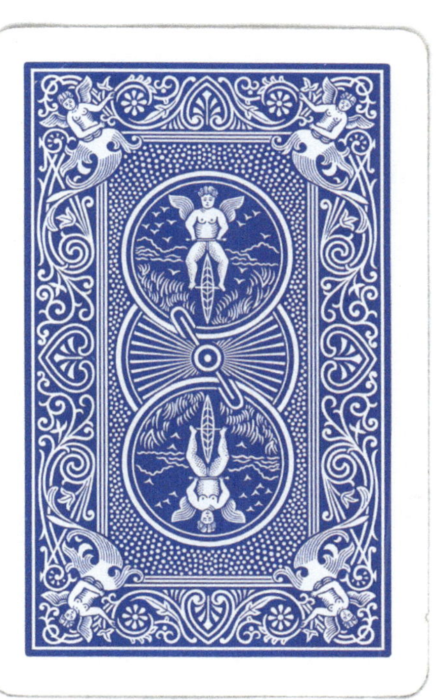

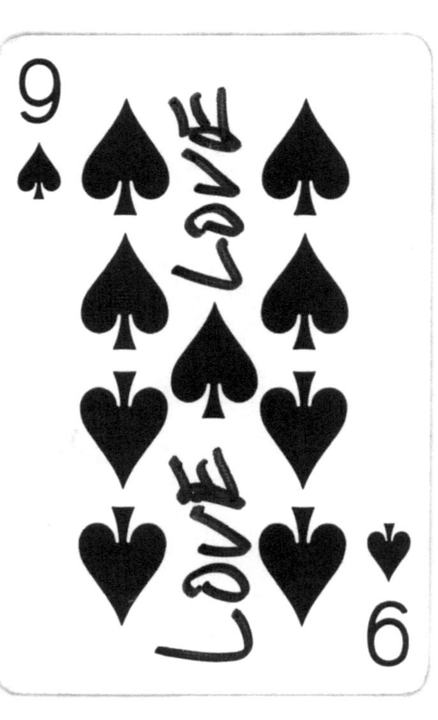
9
LOVE
LOVE
LOVE
LOVE
6

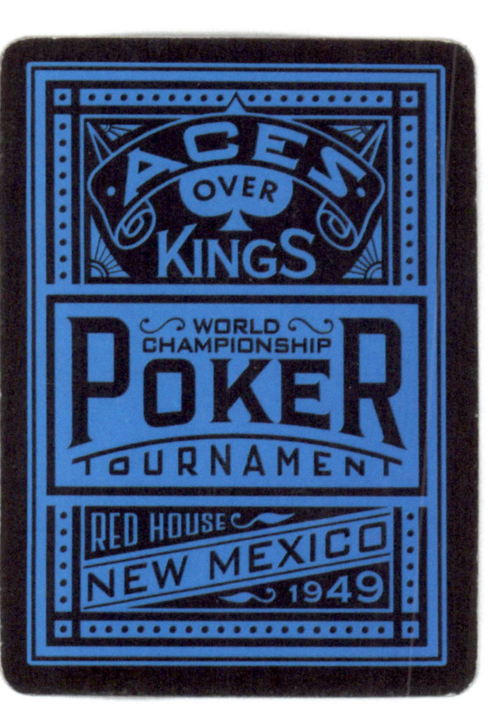

ACES
OVER
KINGS
WORLD
CHAMPIONSHIP
POKER
TOURNAMENT
RED HOUSE
NEW MEXICO
1949

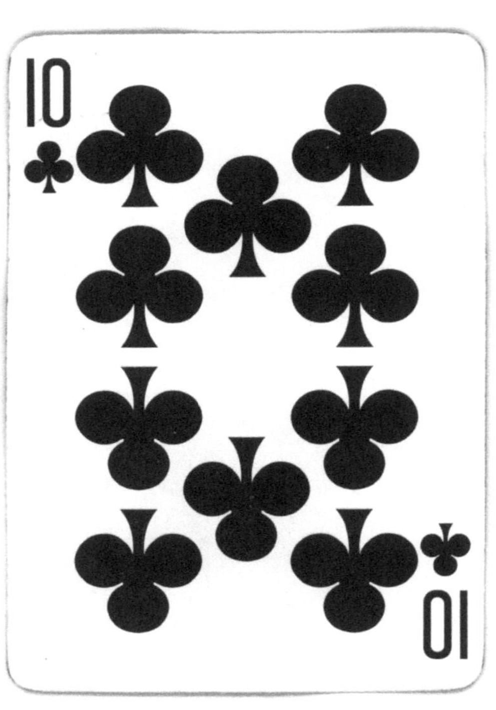

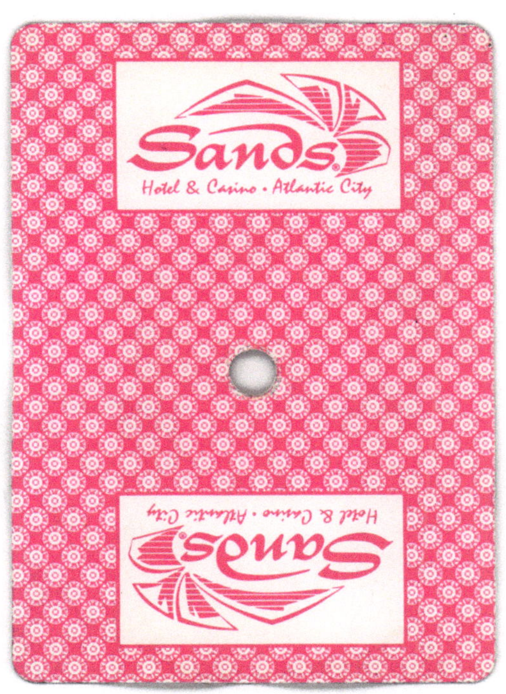

Sands®
Hotel & Casino • Atlantic City
Sands®
Hotel & Casino • Atlantic City

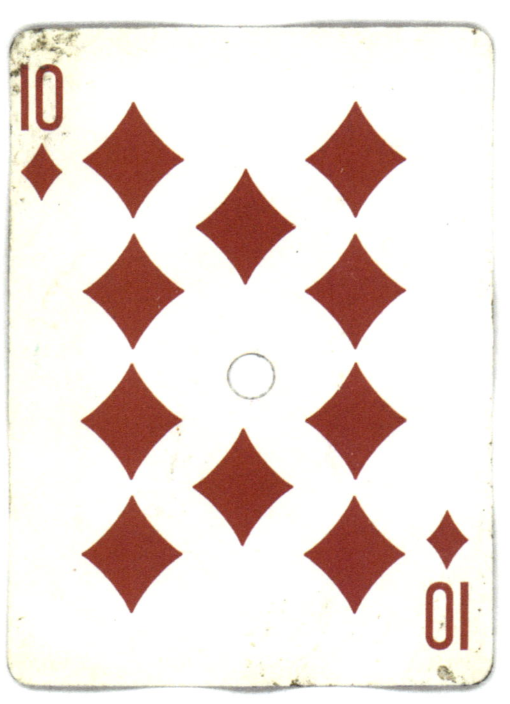

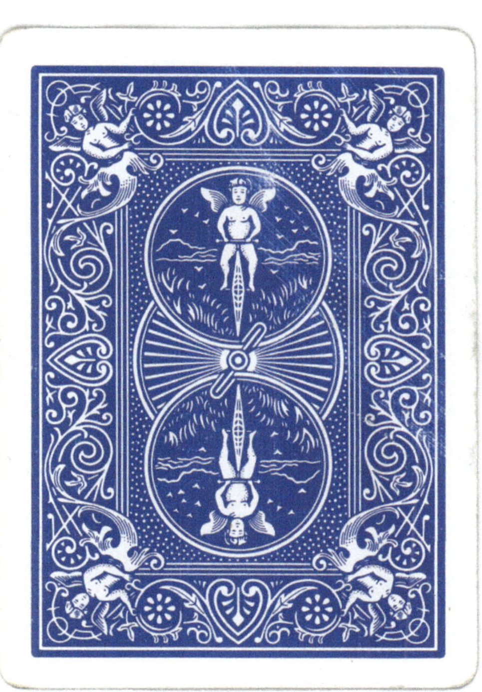

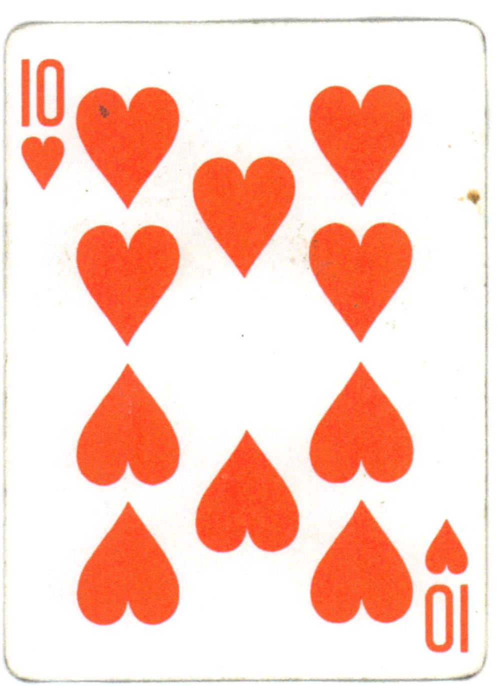

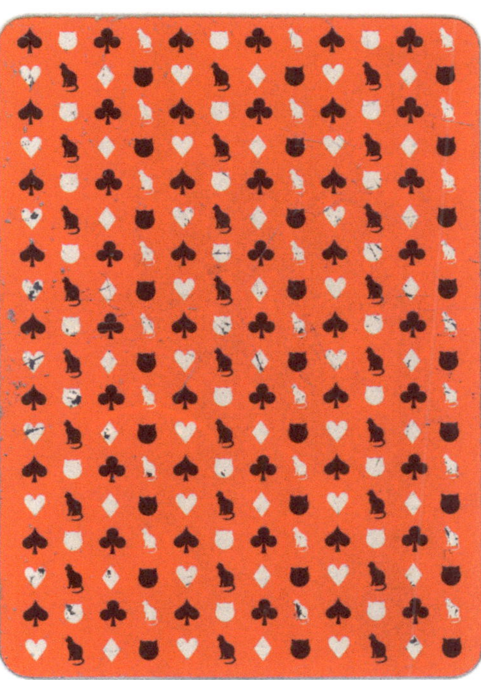

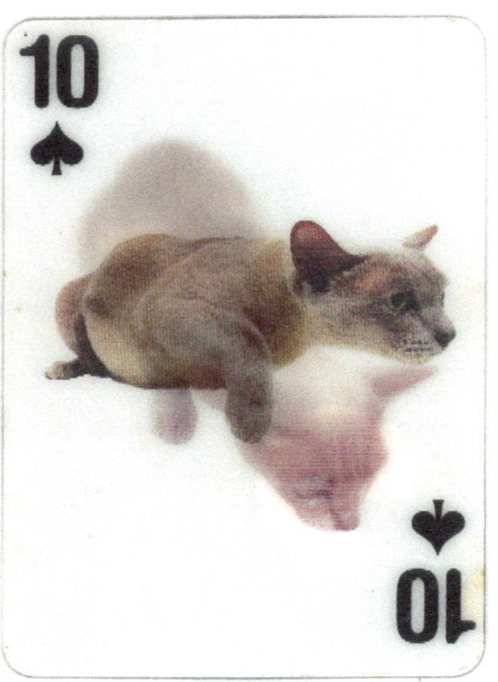
10
♠
10
♠

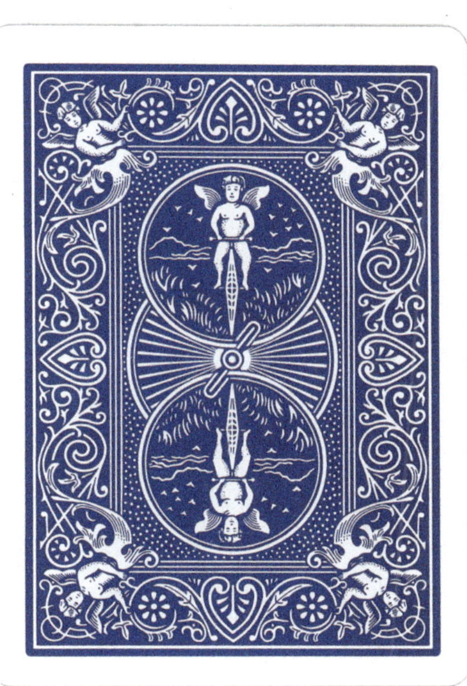

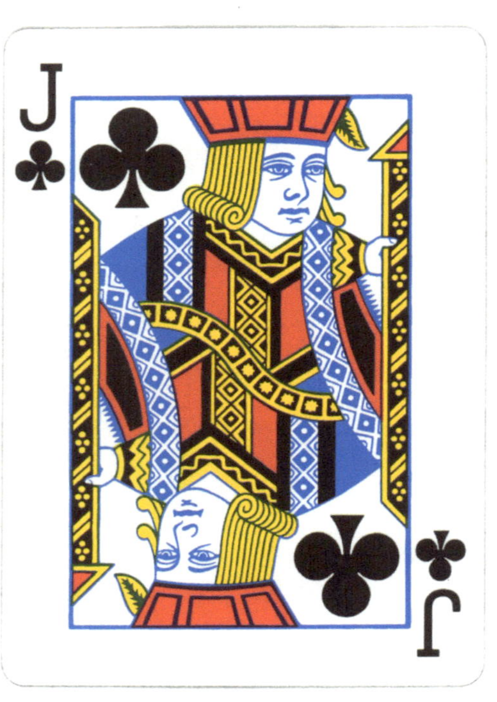

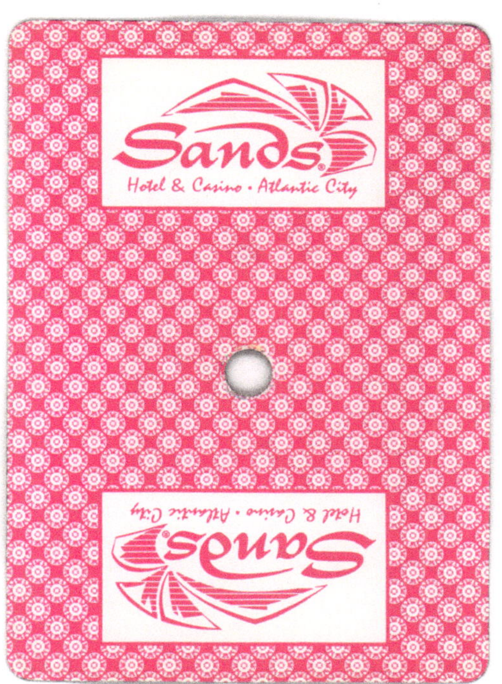

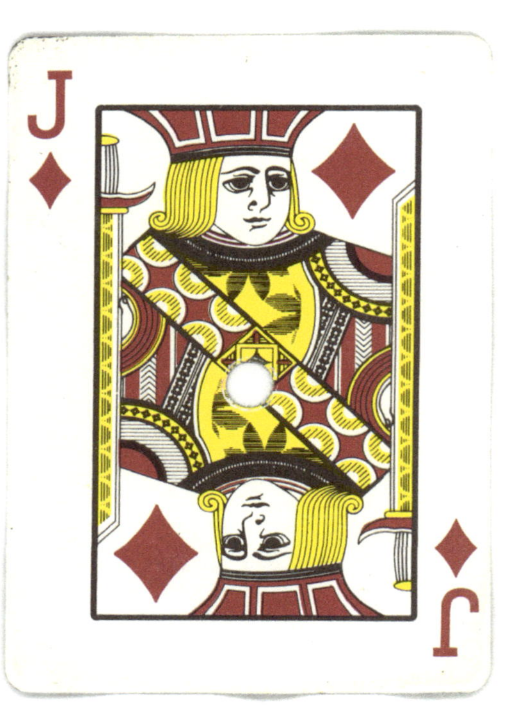

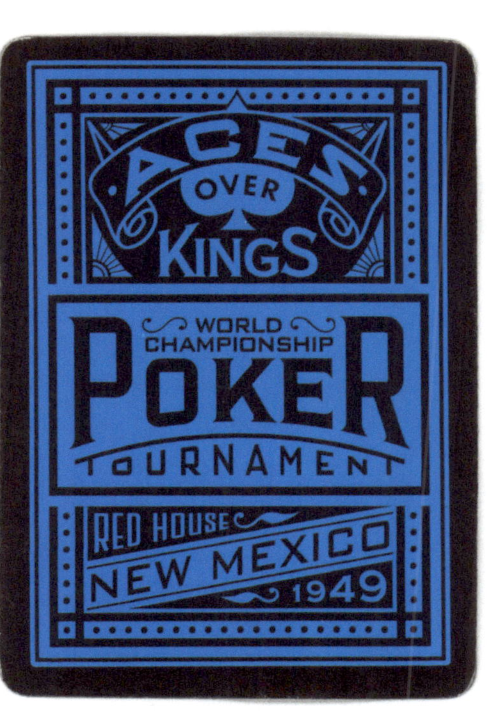
ACES
OVER
KINGS
WORLD
CHAMPIONSHIP
POKER
TOURNAMENT
RED HOUSE
NEW MEXICO
1949

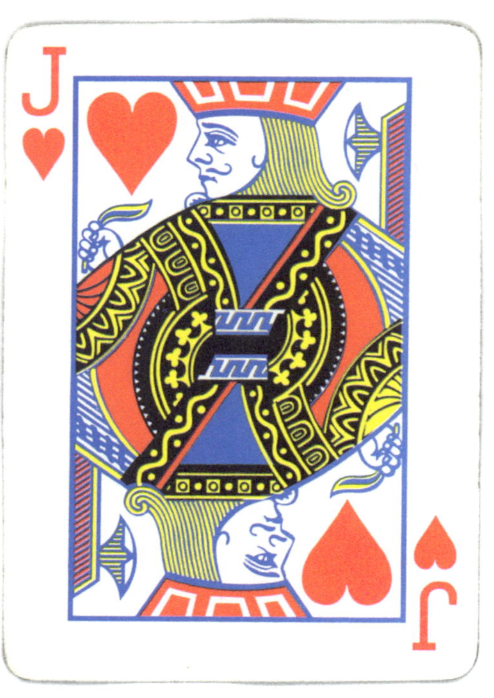

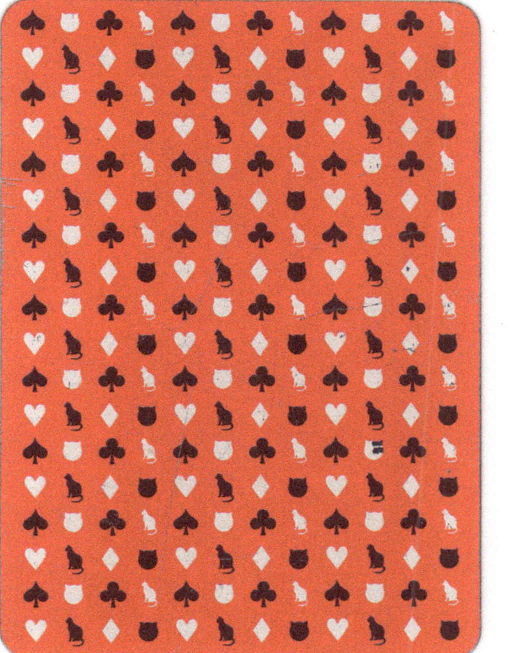

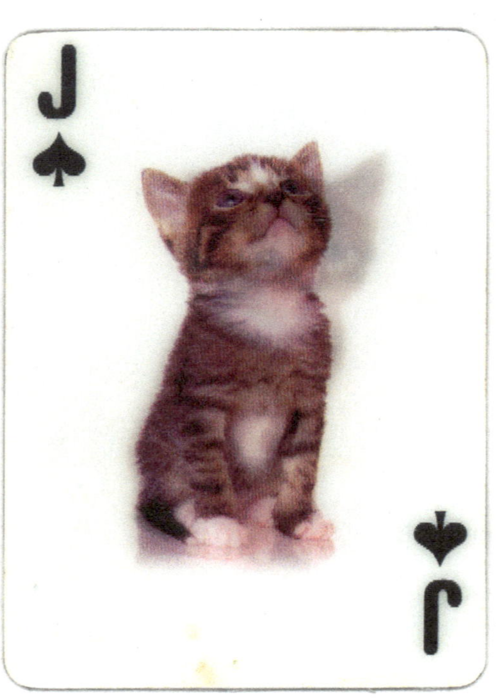

J
♠
♠
ſ

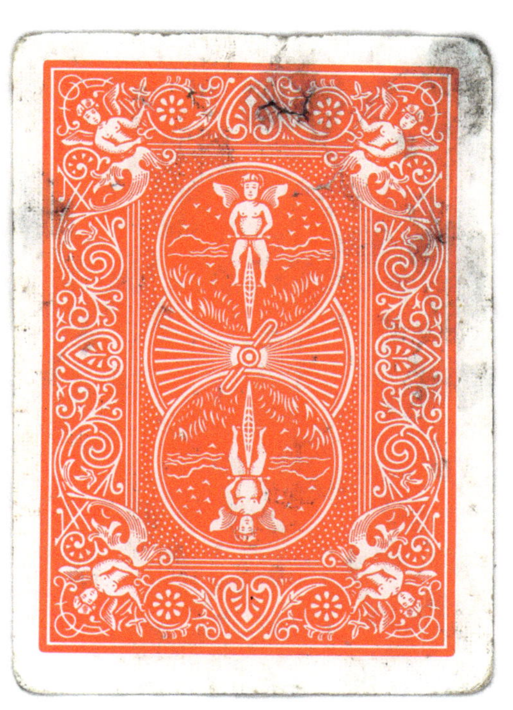

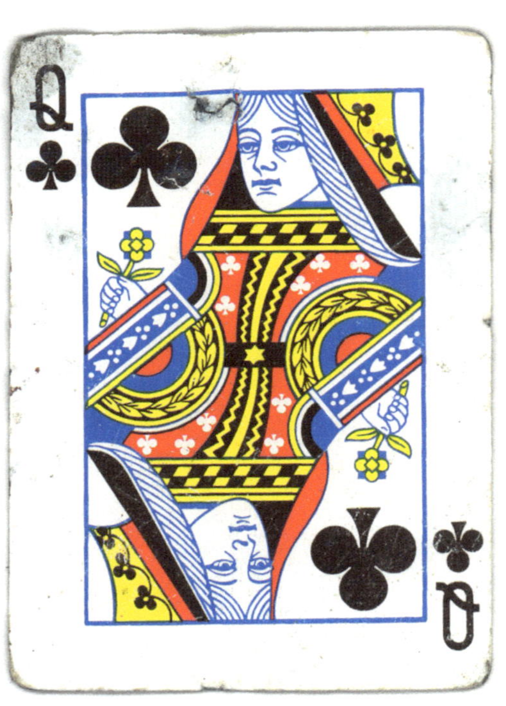

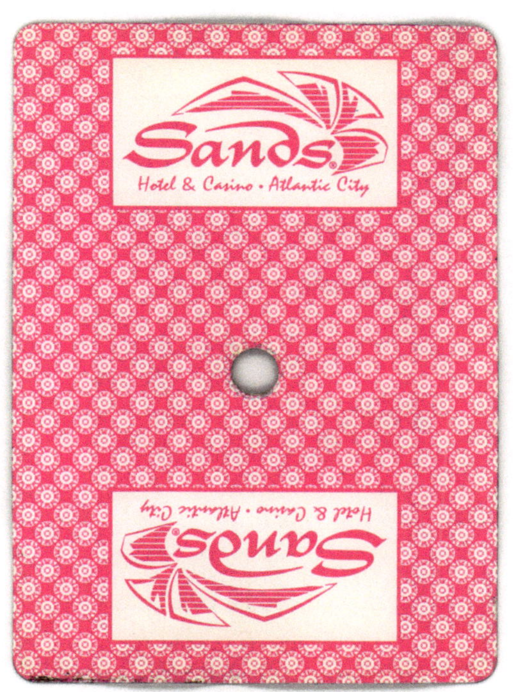
Sands
Hotel & Casino • Atlantic City
Sands
Hotel & Casino • Atlantic City

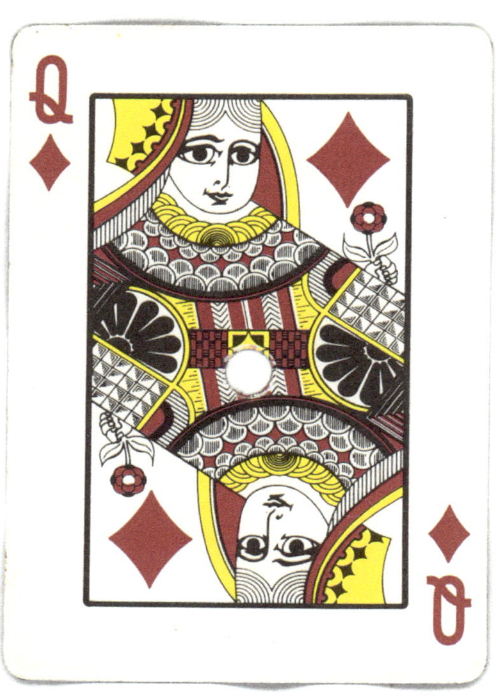

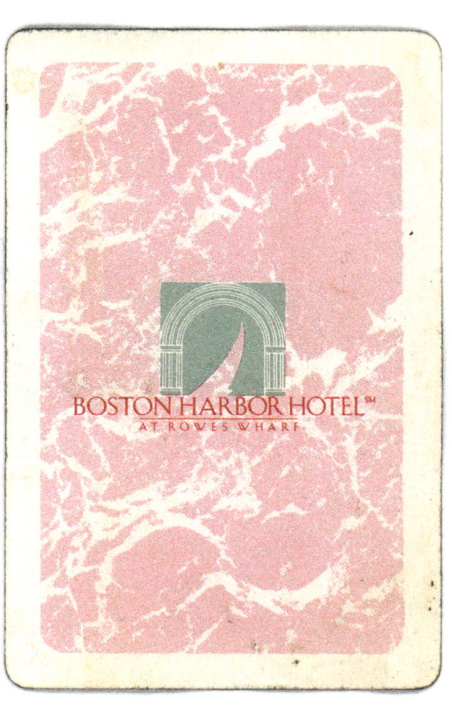
BOSTON HARBOR HOTEL℠
AT ROWES WHARF

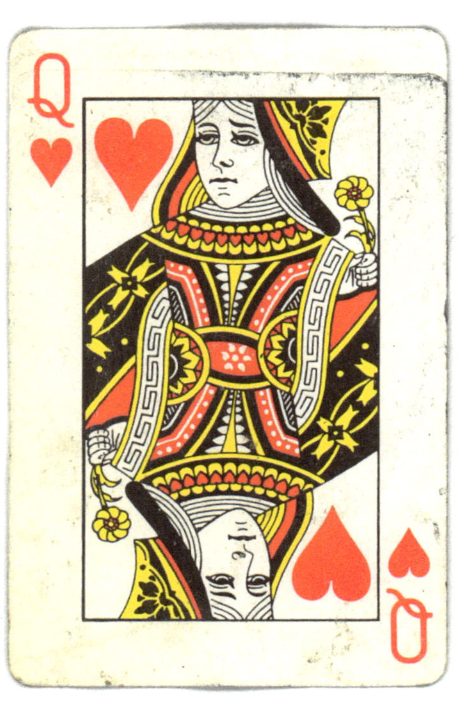

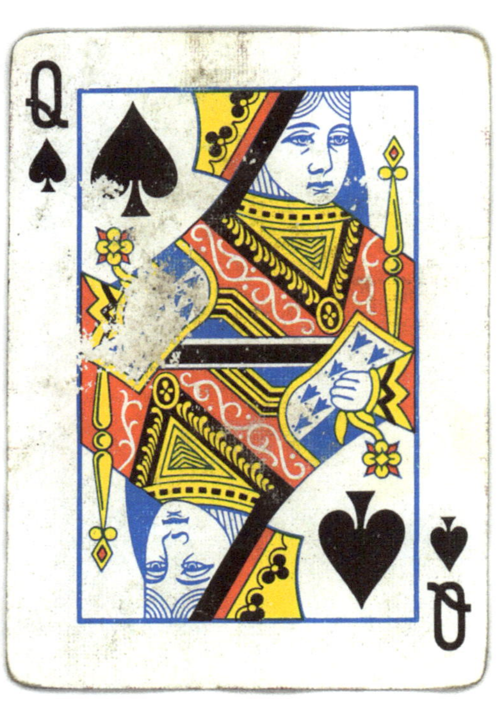

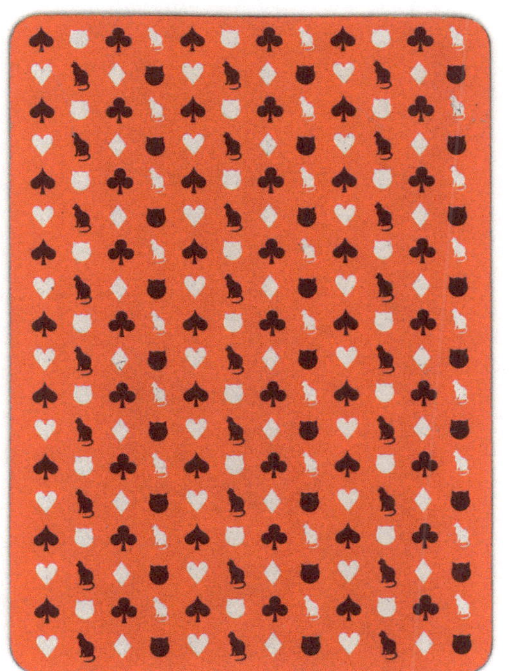

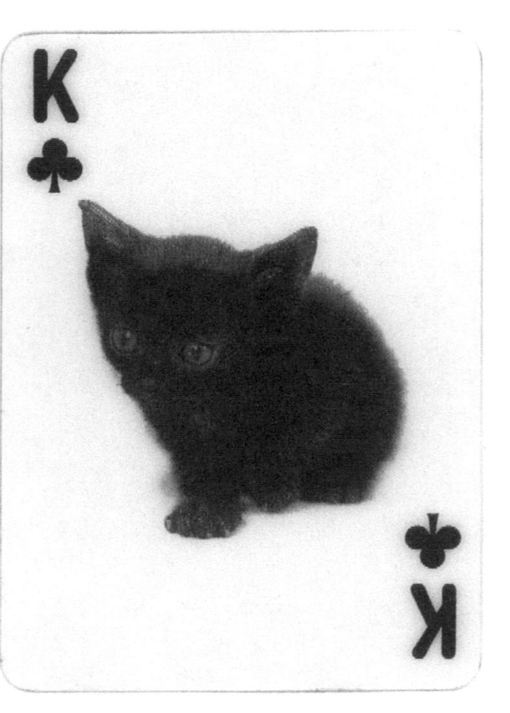

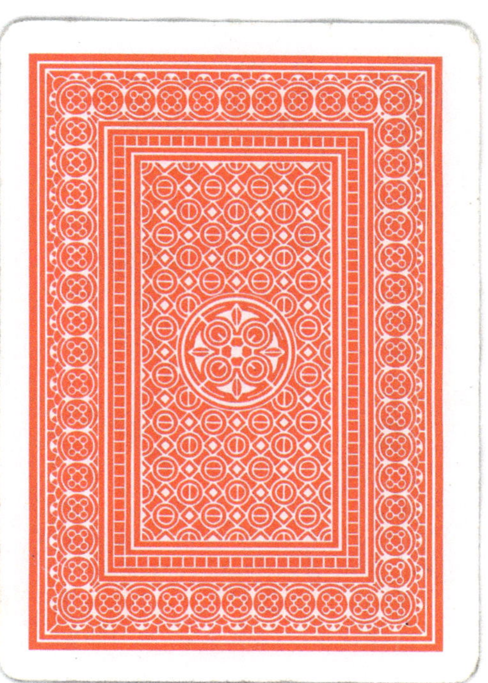

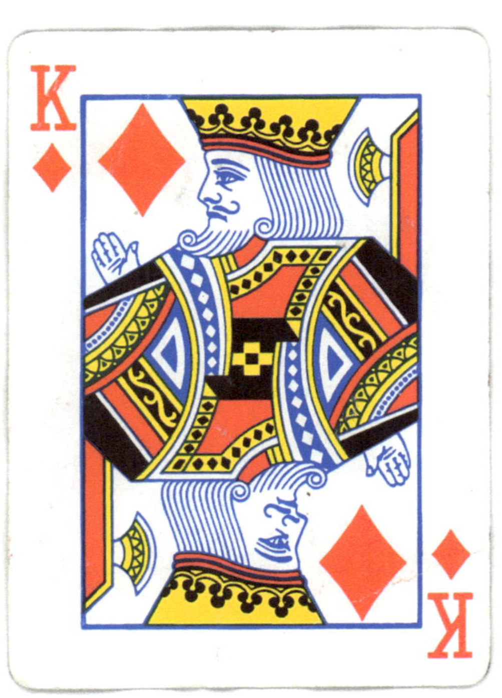

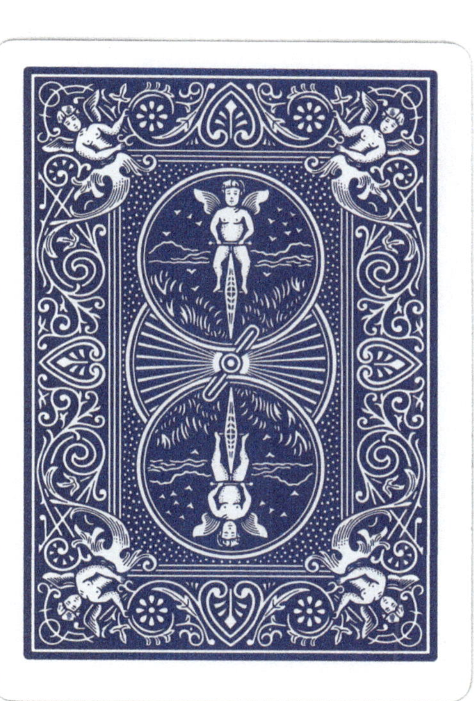

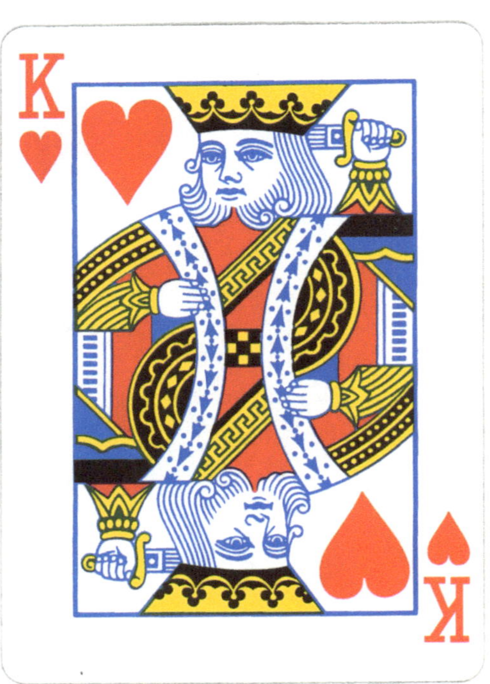

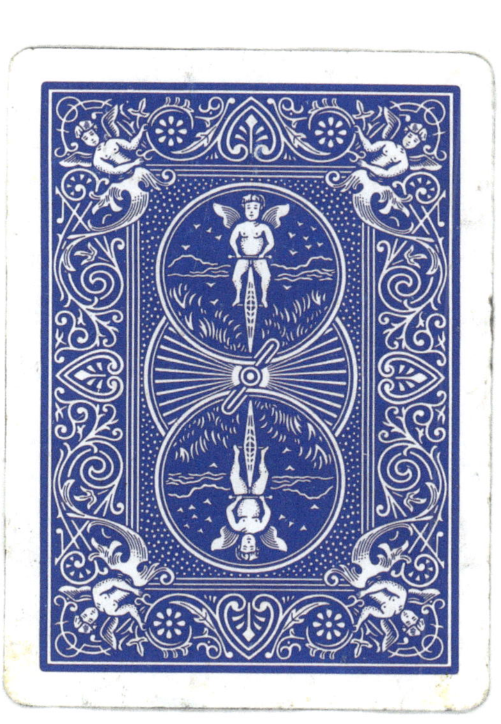

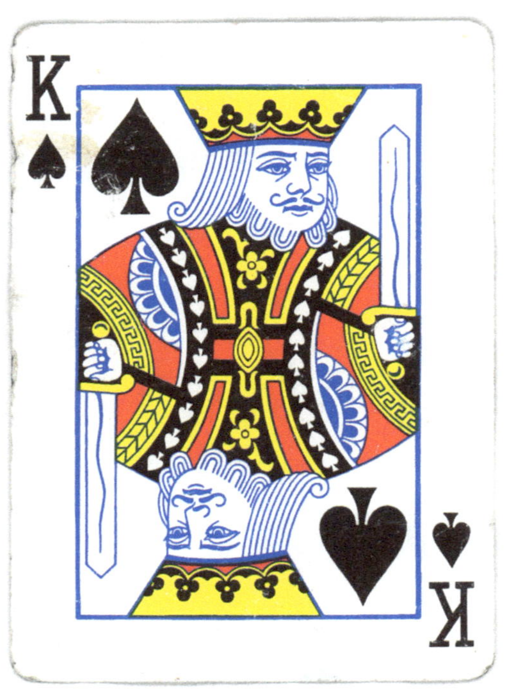

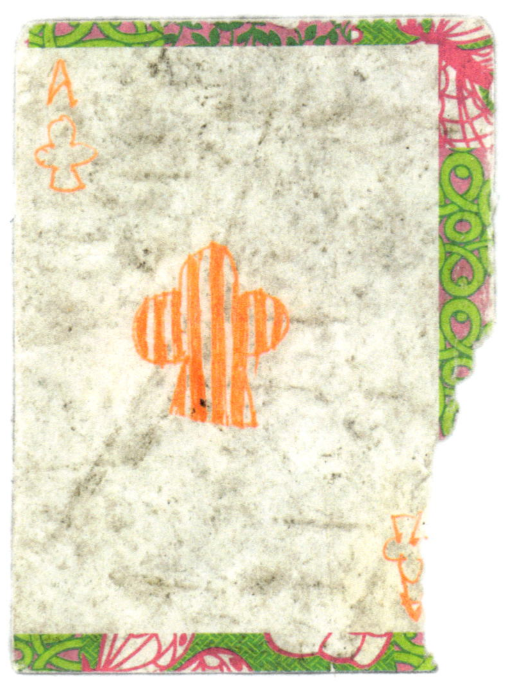

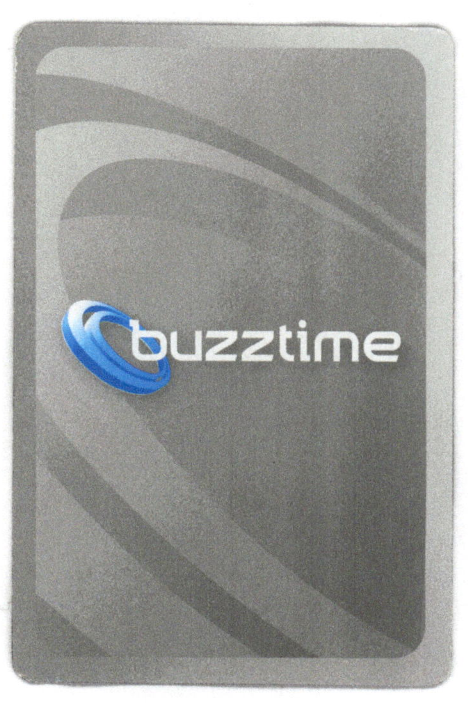

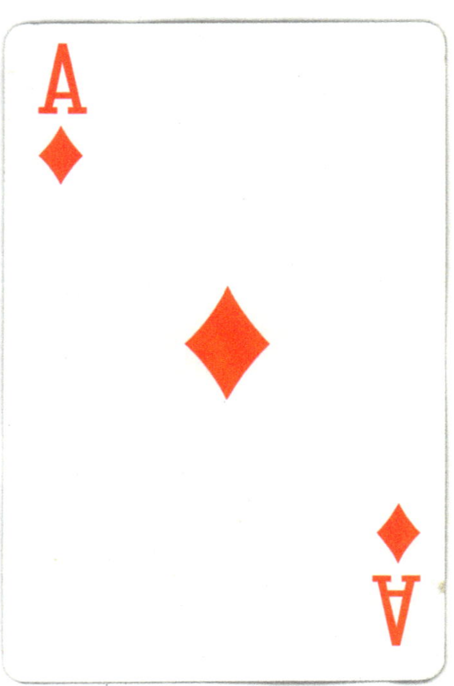

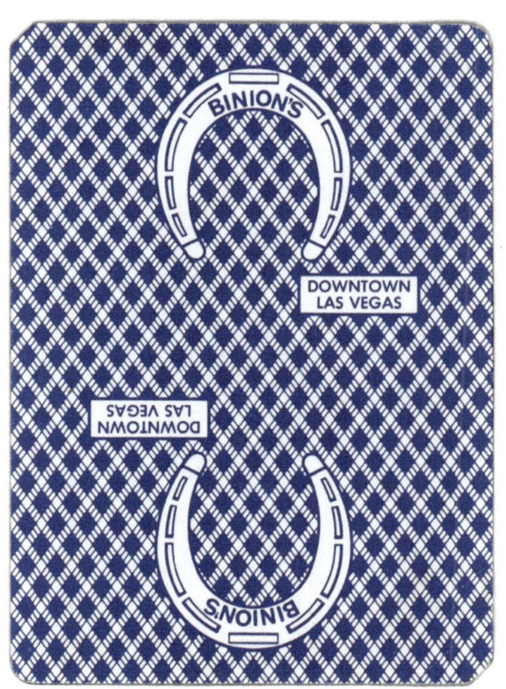

BINION'S
DOWNTOWN
LAS VEGAS

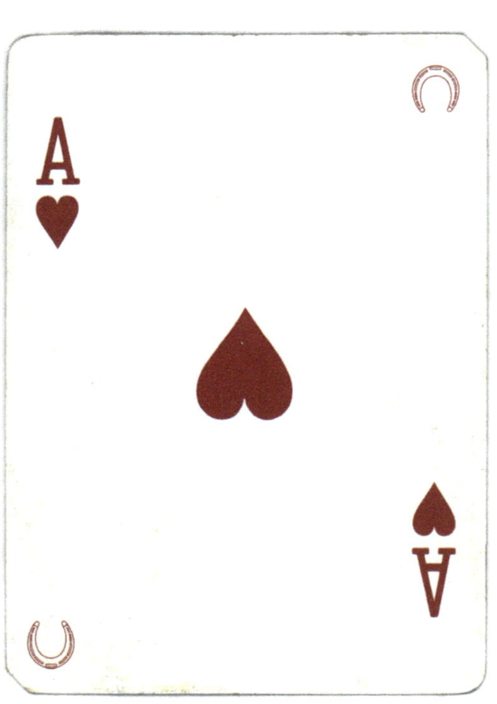

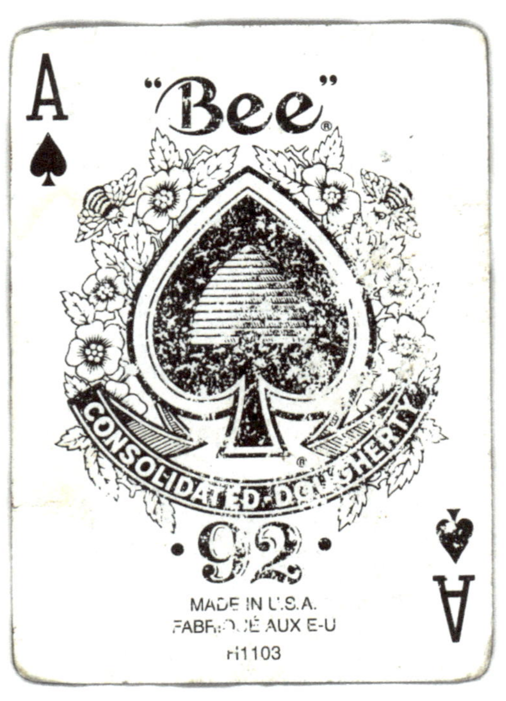
A
"Bee"
CONSOLIDATED DOUGHERTY
92
MADE IN U.S.A.
FABRIQUÉ AUX E-U
H1103
A

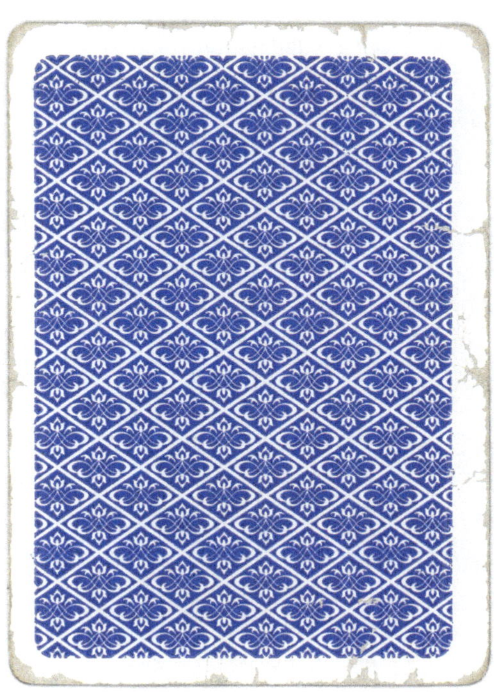

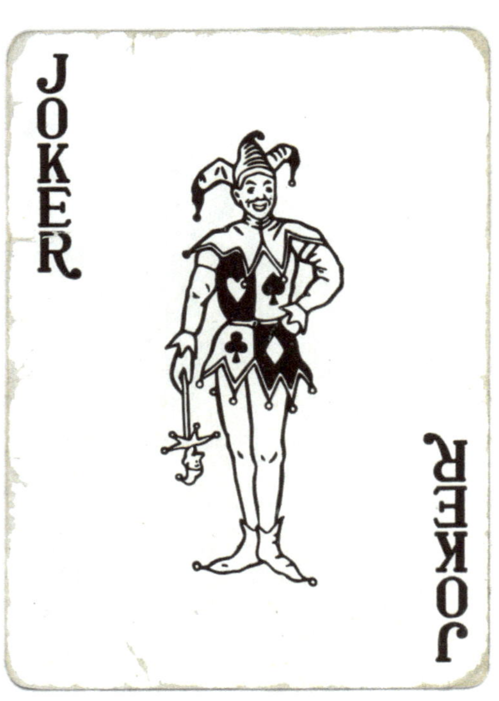
JOKER
JOKER

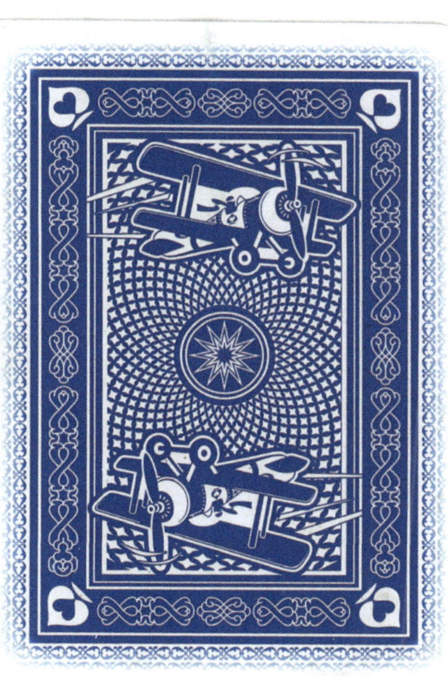

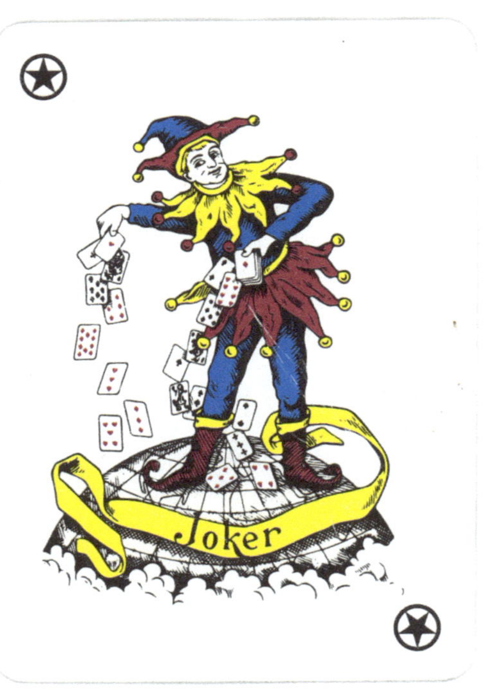

Joker

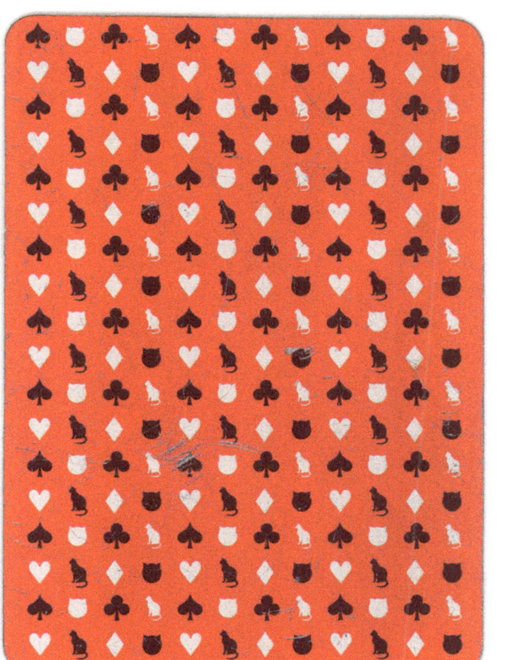

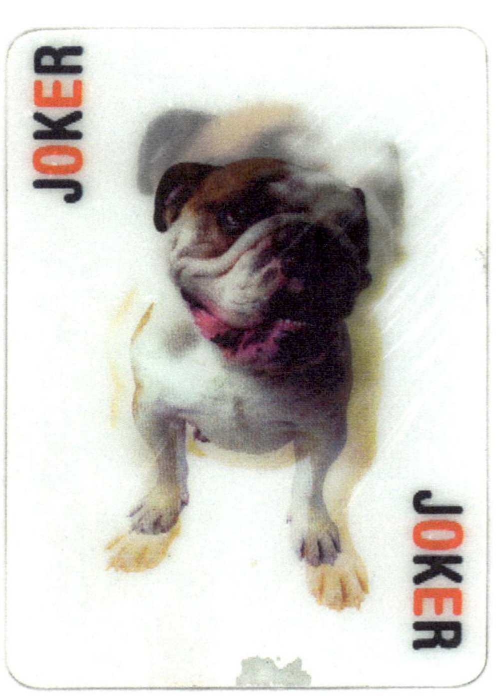
JOKER
JOKER

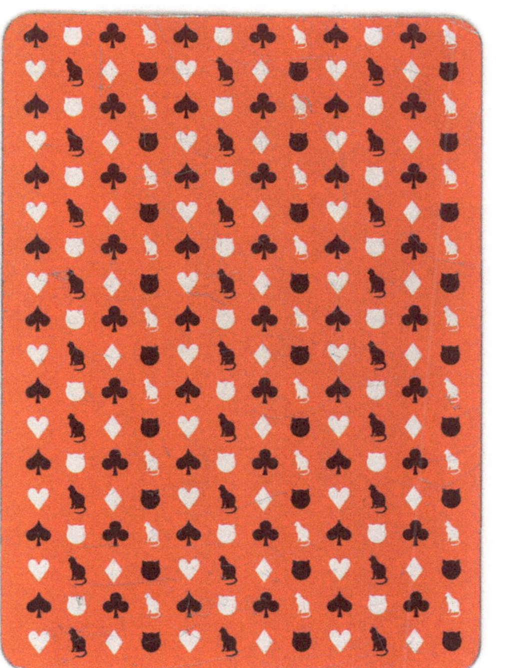

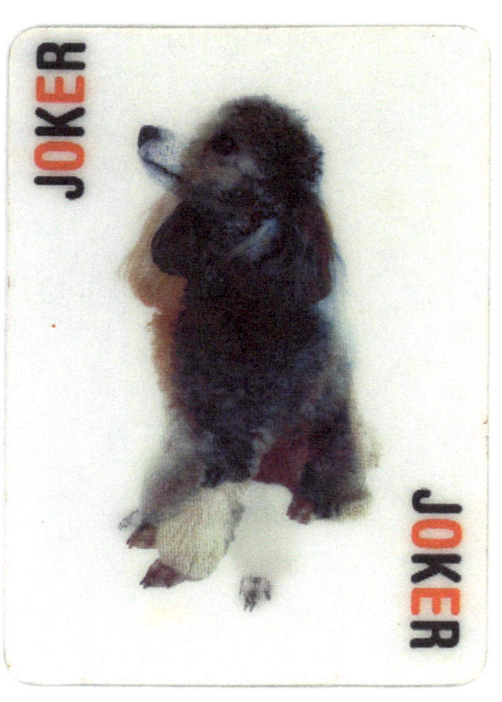

JOKER
JOKER